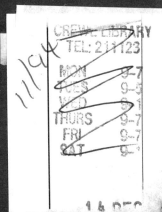

TALL, DARK AND HANSEN

TALL, DARK AND HANSEN
TEN YEARS AT ANFIELD

ALAN HANSEN

WITH

KEN GALLACHER

MAINSTREAM
PUBLISHING

First published in Great Britain in 1988 by
MAINSTREAM PUBLISHING COMPANY (EDINBURGH) LTD
7 Albany Street, Edinburgh EH1 3UC

ISBN 1 85158 089 1 (cloth)
ISBN 1 85158 104 9 (paper)

British Library Cataloguing in Publication Data
Hansen, Alan
    Tall dark and Hansen : ten years at Anfield.
    1. England. Association football.
    Hansen, Alan – Biographies.
    I. Title   II. Gallacher, Ken
    796.334'092'4

ISBN 1-85158-089-1
ISBN 1-85158-104-9 Pbk

Typeset in 11½ on 13½pt Imprint by Bookworm Typesetting, Edinburgh
Printed in Great Britain by Billing & Sons Ltd, Worcester

CONTENTS

For my wife Janet and my children Adam and Lucy.

CHAPTER ONE

Nonsense About a Knee

THERE HAS BEEN a whole load of nonsense talked about my knee and the problems which it has given me down through almost all the years of my career. There is no way that I can claim that everything is perfect but, equally, I want to lay to rest the rumours which have built up whenever I have missed a match or two. Stories went about that I was in constant pain through season 1987-88 when we won the title, that I could not train with the rest of the players at Anfield, and that my career was in danger. There were whispers, too, suggesting that when I did stop playing I could be left a virtual cripple. None of these are true. The problem with my knee started away back when I was playing for Partick Thistle and over the years of constant action it has worsened. There is no doubting that – but not to the extent some people seem to think. In fact, when I had a cartilage removed in the summer of 1988 that was the first important operation I had had on the knee. The basic problem has been simply wear and tear allied to the kind of build I have. I am gangly and long-legged and the doctors have told me that this has added to the problems I have had. But they have also told me that there is nothing seriously wrong with the knee.

9

When I had the cartilage removed, it was done with a 'scope and I was only in hospital for around 48 hours. There is no legacy of pain and I honestly feel as fit as I did five years ago or maybe even longer ago than that.

To be honest, there is no way I would be playing football if I thought that I would be doing myself permanent damage. Nothing would be worth that. Really the only time I have felt it at all recently was when we were doing pre-season training – but that was natural after having the cartilage removed. The problem had been diagnosed as being rather different from the usual cartilage damage. Mine was crushed rather than torn. Usually it is a tear which footballers get but the operation was more or less the same and while it used to be a serious business now it is a whole lot simpler. In fact, a few days after the specialist allowed me home from hospital I was able to go out on the golf course.

Of course, when I was hurt in a pre-season game soon after undergoing the cartilage operation there was a lot more talk about my "injury crisis" but it was a simple injury which you pick up in games. Having said that, I do know that if it had happened to the knee which had just been operated on then my career might well have been over. I don't know if that knee could have stood up to the damage my attempt at a tackle caused.

We were playing in a tournament in La Coruna against Atletico Madrid and the game had only gone about quarter of an hour when one of their forwards broke down the touchline and I went across to tackle him. I went to make the tackle, then pulled out of it a little because I thought I was going to whack him. As I did that my foot stuck in the turf and my whole leg twisted. I heard a crack and before I knew what was happening I was lying on the track in agony. It was really painful when I did it and I had to be carried into the dressing-room. That was on the Friday night and it was the Monday before we were back in Liverpool and I was able to see a specialist. Of course, by this time the injury had become a major crisis in the newspapers and the rumours began to pile up again. But it was a simple

Hansen, skipper of Liverpool in their double winning season and an Anfield regular through a decade of success.

knock, the type players can collect in any match at all and the other knee was perfectly all right.

Because I have played on while suffering from knocks the idea has got around that somehow or other I am injury-prone. But you have only to look at my playing record with Liverpool to see how wrong that view is. I have played in more than 500 games for the club since joining them from Partick Thistle back in the spring of 1977. And, as well as these games, you can add in European matches, cup games and friendly matches. If I had been dogged by injury the way it has been suggested then I would never have been able to reach that games total. It would have been out of the question.

I wouldn't have survived long enough to get the testimonial match the club granted me in the summer of 1988. That was a terrific night for me. England manager Bobby Robson brought his international squad to play against my Liverpool team at Anfield and the fans who have been so good to me in my Liverpool career turned out to give me a memorable night. I'll never forget that. I have always liked to think that my relationship with the supporters has been a good one and that night helped to prove that. Ever since I moved to Liverpool I have been struck by the Scouse humour and by the way the rival fans can get on with each other without any trouble. It was never that way in Glasgow where I played my football before. You just wouldn't find Rangers and Celtic fans sitting in the pub together after a match – but that happens in Liverpool. In fact it's one of the things I love about Merseyside. When I first came down to join the club I can remember going with Terry Mac for a pint or two after a game and you could do it without any fuss or bother, without worrying if there was going to be trouble. You would find the rival fans in the same pub, drinking with each other, joking with each other – just the way it should be. Sure, there would be some banter between them. They would make jokes about each other but then they would laugh at the jokes together. They even go together to the derby games. When we have played against Everton at Wembley we have had rival fans travelling in the same cars or buses to

Alan Hansen edges ahead of Crystal Palace's Ian Walsh. Palace were one of the London teams who flopped in a title challenge.

London for the big match. I don't believe that you would get that situation anywhere else in the world. You certainly would never have Rangers and Celtic fans travelling on the same bus to an Old Firm game. And I doubt if Real Madrid and Atletico Madrid fans would do it. Or the rival supporters of Inter and AC Milan in Italy. But it's OK on Merseyside and it's always made my feelings for the fans even stronger than they might have been.

Of course I owe them a lot for the way they welcomed me to the club and the way they supported me all the way through those hundreds of games. But I owe them for something else, too – the title of this book. It was a group of Liverpool fans who had a banner at one of the games which read "Tall, Dark and Hansen" – so I've pinched it for this book. I hope they don't mind – and whoever thought it up, thanks. I only hope that I'll be seeing that banner and maybe a whole lot more fluttering on the Kop for a few seasons to come.

As I said earlier I feel as fit as I have ever done and I'll play on for as long as Kenny Dalglish wants me to. It would have been fine, too, if Andy Roxburgh had been able to consider me for that game in Oslo which Scotland won 2-1. It was the beginning of yet another World Cup campaign. Unhappily, though, I had been injured over in Spain. While I thought I would be ignored after my brief comeback when Andy Roxburgh took over, there is always something inside you which keeps you hoping that you will play for your country again. I would love to be involved again. It's always important to play for your country – and I was never able to play often enough for my own liking. It's also another arena to test your skills in. It's your chance to face up to some of the world's best players and, with English clubs banned from Europe still, we don't have that opportunity at club level any more. You have the odd game pre-season. Or you can play in challenge games. Neither of these is any substitute for the European Cup. Maybe if I am picked for Scotland I'll get the chance, once more, to play at that level. I doubt, the way things are going, that I will do so again for the club. The European Union ban on English clubs

All the pride in being Liverpool's so successful captain is shown here as Alan Hansen raises the League Championship trophy high in the air in triumph after yet another title win for the Mersey machine.

remains and there are few signs that they will lift it in the near future. We can all hope that they do but I'm fairly certain it would come too late to allow me to be involved.

So, maybe with Scotland, I'll get a chance again. If Andy Roxburgh does ask me I'll be able to tell him exactly what I've told all of you here– that I am 100 per cent fit. That my knee gives me no problems. That I train with the other lads at Anfield and do exactly what they do. That the close season operation ended the nagging knee problem which had troubled me on and off for a season.

Like I say, the injury has never been as serious as some people have suggested. I am simply another victim of the demands made on footballers in these modern times. "Wear and tear" was the doctor's summing up and what it meant was playing 70 or 80 games in a season at the highest level possible.

Alan Hansen and his wife Janet relax over a champagne meal.

No one was asked to play as many games as that in the past – but when you are with a team as successful as Liverpool have been during my years with them then you are talking of an enormous amount of matches simply because they *are* so successful. You have the usual League games, which everyone plays, but with a top club you are also looking at League Cup and FA Cup ties which mount up the more success you have. Also there were the years in Europe and when you are talking about winning the European Cup then you are adding another nine games to the season's tally.

Still, I wouldn't have had it any other way. The games have been good. The rewards have been high. And the friendships I have made at the club have been valued by me. It seems strange to look back and think of the times when I played for Partick Thistle in front of a few thousand loyal Firhill fans. Stranger still to look back even further and remember coming straight from the golf course to play for Sauchie Juniors when the game was not as high a priority as it has become at Liverpool. Now, after all these years and all these medals, I am the senior member of the squad and the club captain. It's a satisfying feeling and it's a responsibility that I can't take lightly. Captaining the best club in Britain is an honour I never imagined I would earn.

CHAPTER TWO

When Soccer Came Second

AFTER THE YEARS with Liverpool, those years with a club where professionalism is a key word and where winning becomes a way of life, it's hard to recall the days when football didn't mean everything to me. But that was the case when I was a youngster and still at school in Sauchie, the village in Stirlingshire where I was born and grew up.

Golf was more important to me then. If I had the choice of going out on to the golf course or playing for the local football team then the football came a poor second. There was even a spell when I believed that I might just be able to make the grade as a professional golfer. It would have been a much more enticing prospect, at that time, than playing football. The game wasn't that important to me at all. I gave it up three or four times when I was a teenager. I don't know why – don't ask me about it because I would find it impossible to explain the reasons. Looking back now it doesn't seem possible, even to me, that I would have relegated football to second place so readily.

To some extent it was circumstances surrounding the local team which kept bringing me back to the game. It wasn't that I missed playing – it was more that the team would be needing me. Not because they couldn't do without me as a player – mainly because they had to get someone to make up the numbers. The other lads would come round to the house and they would talk me into playing. Because I didn't want to let down any of my mates I would go back and turn out for them in a game and that would be that until the next time I chucked it. That went on for a long time. I sometimes wonder why my mates bothered with me. Now, of course, I'm glad they did. If they had not kept persuading me to play for the local under-18 team then the career I have enjoyed with Liverpool would simply never have happened.

Even when they did get me back playing it was always on the same condition – and that was that my golf came first. I wouldn't have had it any other way. The guys who ran the team and the lads who played in the team accepted that from me. So on a Saturday you would often see me finish a medal round of golf on the local course, and then come off the 18th green and head straight to the football pitch. Luckily it was right beside the last hole and so I would be there maybe for just after the kick-off. It was a bonus if I made the start of these games.

They worked out a special little system to suit me. If my round of golf was not going to finish until after the game kicked off they would name me as substitute. Then, when I got to the ground and changed, they would take off one of the players and push me on. This was for the Sauchie under-18 team and it still amazes me that they were willing to go along with that kind of bizarre arrangement. If they hadn't been then I suppose my football career would have been over before it had started properly.

I played for the school team, too. It was a good side and I enjoyed their matches. For a spell I was playing for the school team in the morning and then the under-18 team in the afternoon. That was when there was no golf – in the darkest days of winter. The rest of the time 18 holes had to be fitted in most Saturdays. In fact there were occasions when I was trying to play 36 holes because I would become involved with tournaments at the club. There were county games, too, and medals. At times it was difficult for me to fit in the football as well. I loved golf. I still do to a certain extent, although my chances of playing are distinctly limited. There isn't too much golf allowed at Liverpool during the football season so all my playing – or almost all of it – has to be telescoped into the summer months.

When I was a youngster I used to love summer coming round. I'd be off school and there would be golf seven days a week for the whole six weeks of the summer holidays. That was my idea of heaven. Eventually I became good enough to get my handicap down to two – it was that when I was with Thistle and still that when I moved south to sign for Liverpool. But I could never get it any lower than two, possibly because once I signed for Partick Thistle and decided that football offered me a good career, then golf had to take a little bit of a back seat. If you are training hard and playing hard and you have all the demands of professional football to face once or maybe twice a week, then you simply don't have the chance of maintaining the high standards needed to whittle down your handicap. I joined the Hillside club at Southport where I now stay, but because I can't find the time to play in club medals I don't have an official handicap. I reckon I play to around six or eight nowadays but my appearances at the course are almost exclusively confined to the summer when the football season has ended. I still try to play quite a bit then but in winter golf is out. And with the close season being so short you can imagine just how little golf I now play during a year.

My best golf performance was probably in the Scottish Boys Championship which I qualified to play in one year. It was a stroke play tournament and it was played at Montrose that time. I shot rounds of 75, 73, 72, 72 for a 72-hole total of 292. I was delighted with that and it was good enough to see me finish in seventh place. But it wasn't good enough to suggest that golf would give me a livelihood when I left school at 18. I came out of school with four A-levels and seven O-levels – and not a thought in my head about what I was going to do for the rest of my life.

To some extent that is when football stepped in to save me. I honestly had not a clue about what I wanted to do. To start with I drifted into a job with an insurance company. I had the qualifications from school for a good job there and I was offered a job in their Stirling office. On the surface it looked OK. The prospects were good, the money wasn't bad and I knew that I could handle the work. It would have been a job I could have stayed in for the rest of my life. But, somehow, it wasn't for me.

The skipper on the Kop. But this was when he signed from Partick Thistle for a £100,000 fee and took his first look at Anfield.

I could not handle the nine-to-five routine of office work and eventually when they sent me on a course to their head office in Perth I cracked. I had been there just over five weeks when this course came up and I lasted on it just one day. One single day was all I could cope with.

I came back on the train to Stirling that night with one of the directors of the company who was travelling back to Glasgow. The local manager had explained to him that I had only been on the course for a day and was already wanting to get home and they didn't seem able to understand this attitude. I don't think they had any idea how I felt but deep down I knew that I just would never be able to hold down that type of job. I saw all the years stretching away in front of me and I couldn't visualise myself sitting at a desk doing the same kind of thing day after day, week after week, month after month and year after year. Millions of people can do that. Millions of people enjoy that. But I knew I wasn't cut out to be one of them. I knew that I needed something different and I did have the chance to join Partick Thistle at this time. That was my escape route.

I can remember on that train back from Perth explaining this to the director and he said to me: "So, you want to play football, do you? Well, if that's what you decide I hope I can look forward to seeing your name in the newspapers in the years to come." I've thought about that often and I've wondered, too, if he has seen my name and if he has pieced together the fact that the teenager on the train who was leaving his company did eventually make something of himself as a footballer.

Funnily enough, it was not a great desire on my part to become a professional footballer that saw me sign for Thistle. Nor was it some romantic notion that I should join the Firhill club because my brother, John, was already playing there. Like so many of the things that have happened to me in my life it was all a little bit of an accident.

I had trained with Thistle when I was 15 and again when I was 16 and 17 and they had been keen to sign me. But I wasn't all that interested then. Plus, my father was always convinced that I had a great talent and he was waiting for one of the bigger clubs, one of the glamorous clubs, to come along and sign me. All those times when I trained with them for a little spell he would advise me against signing for them. He did that until the time came when I was offered another chance to sign and I knew that this was going to be better than an insurance office!

Actually Thistle had some kind of tie-up with the Sauchie club. It was used almost as a kind of nursery for the Glasgow team and they often came out to play practice games against us. I remember there was some kind of special game one Sunday and as usual I had spent the morning on the golf course, finished my round, cut across to the football ground straight from the 18th green, changed into my football gear and gone on to the field to play against them.

Early days and Hansen finds himself in the opposition penalty box backed up by fellow defender Joey Jones. The goalkeeper is another Scot, Dave Stewart of Leeds United.

The Thistle manager at that time was Dave McParland who had been with the club as a player and was now boss. He knew all about me. He had seen me before and he had wanted to sign me. This time I think I must really have impressed him. I was in midfield, which was always the role I played then, and I stuck a few decent passes around. I must have played better than I thought I had because the next day he was knocking on the front door of the house and offering me terms.

Thistle offered me £250 as a lump signing-on fee – if someone else had come along and offered me 50 quid more then I would have joined them. It wasn't a case of wanting to play for Thistle particularly, it was a way out of my career dilemma. I had no money then and I knew I was going nowhere fast either in my life or in my job. That's why, though Falkirk were also interested, I took the chance and started off on the career which was to finish up here at Anfield.

I suppose I went to Thistle because nothing better came along. The scouts from the bigger clubs didn't share my dad's high opinion of my talents back then. So Dave McParland took me under his wing and converted me into a defender. He was the first to do that – and it was a position I just didn't want to play. I had never played anywhere else but in midfield and there was no way I wanted to change – especially by being sent back into defence. But when I arrived at Thistle and started to play in a game, within half an hour Dave McParland had ordered me to go back to the centre of the defence. I wasn't happy at all. I just had no inclination to play back there – in fact, I didn't believe that I could play there.

That tells you just how much I knew at the time! I mean, I couldn't understand why anyone would want me to play there. I thought he must be crazy. For a start I couldn't tackle. Also, although I was six feet two inches tall, I was very ordinary in the air. Before shooting up in height I'd been more like a winger, playing on the left-hand side of midfield, getting the ball and playing it and trying to put a few decent passes around. I'd never tried to head the ball – and I'd never even thought about playing in defence. But Dave McParland must have seen something in me that even I didn't realise I had. He recognised that I could read the game. Although I hadn't realised it, this was one of my major assets and it has remained one of them right through to the present day. It was always there, just something that I must have had naturally, and it carried me

An anxious-looking Alan Hansen brings an awkward ball under control.

through. It took signing for Thistle and the perception of Dave McParland to see it and to a large extent he has to be one of the men responsible for any kind of success I've had in the game. It was a blow to me when he left a year or so after he signed me. He was offered a job with Celtic as assistant manager to Jock Stein and it was clearly too good a chance to turn down. He moved on and Bertie Auld, one of the Lisbon Lions from Celtic's famous European Cup win, took over.

From then until the day I left after being sold to Liverpool I suffered some of my unhappiest times in the game. Bertie and I just didn't get on. Over the years he did a good job for Thistle, always seeming to be able to keep them in the Premier League, but the way he did it left a lot to be desired. In the end I was glad to get away.

CHAPTER THREE

Rows with Bertie and a Burst Appendix

UNDER THE GUIDANCE of Dave McParland before his departure for Celtic I had been gradually improving the defensive side of my game. My heading improved and though I'm still not the best in the air I can handle situations there. When you have height on your side then you have chances. Also the game was taking place in front of me and with the knack of reading situations which Dave McParland had spotted I found myself able to see things happening early and be prepared for the opposition moves when they came. I was also that bit quicker than a lot of people gave me credit for. A few managers had the opinion that I lacked pace but really I had a long stride and that deceived a lot of people. With full-time training I was even able to move myself a little bit quicker.

My first-team debut, though, ended with one of my famous pass backs – the kind of pass back which gifts the opposition a goal. This time it was against Dundee and we lost 4-0 at Firhill. My contribution was a pass back to Alan Rough from the 18-yard line. Roughie had taken a goal kick and sent it to me at the edge of the penalty box. I thought I was in the clear and I casually stroked the ball back towards him. In nipped Gordon

Wallace to score and that brought my first-team career to an abrupt end for some time. I didn't get any stick from the manager – though I probably should have done – in fact, he said that I had played quite well. However, when the team was named for the next game I wasn't in it. Nor did I get back for a long time. I vanished without trace.

To some extent, however, my omission was doing me a favour. I had stretched quite suddenly in height and I was six feet two inches tall – but only eleven and a half stones in weight. I was incredibly weak for football at this level. It was quite a handicap for me when I was starting off at Firhill. I just didn't have the strength to compete properly. It plagued me for a fair period of time and probably held back my career. Managers have admitted that they looked at me in my early days with Thistle and were put off signing me because of my lack of strength. Ian Greaves was at Bolton when he contemplated signing me. Jimmy Armfield was boss at Leeds when he was close to putting in a bid and Newcastle United also expressed some interest and came to look at me. All of them have since admitted that they didn't go for me because I looked too weak to stand up to the rigours of the English First Division. They were right. I know only too well myself just how right they were – because I was finding it hard to cope with the Scottish Premier League and the demands made on me there.

None of these managers was willing to take a chance on me. They all thought, too, that I seemed too slow for the English game. Mind you, they have since qualified that by pointing out what I knew already, that my long stride gives that appearance. But being too light for my frame was something which troubled me for quite a time. When I moved to Liverpool I reached a fighting weight of 13 stones and over ten years that has scarcely altered by more than a couple of pounds.

Anyhow, the lack of strength and the dreadful pass back apart, I enjoyed learning the new role of central defender. I had a few hairy moments when my positional sense let me down but it was a role I began to feel more comfortable in. I was also enjoying the times with Thistle. There was a kind of family

Alan's boss at Firhill, Bertie Auld, who did his best to make life hell.

feeling about the club and there were a good bunch of lads in the dressing-room. Also, my older brother, John, was able to take me under his wing a little bit when I first joined the club.

But the happy days ended for me when Bertie took over. And, if truth be told, they probably ended for quite a few of the other players too. I'm not going to argue about the results he got. They speak for themselves and they speak for him too. As a manager for Partick Thistle he was successful. He made it difficult for other teams who played against us because he concentrated so much on defensive strategies. It became a bit of a joke among the other players in the Premier League as to how many central defenders Bertie might play in any one game. We regularly had three – Jackie Campbell, myself and Andy Anderson. But I can remember playing in the team for one game when he had *five* centre-backs on the field.

Anyhow, as I said, he had a limited success with Thistle and he was certainly able to keep them clear of relegation for season after season. But don't ask me to commend the way he did it. He ruled Firhill by fear. He got away with it because he got results and so the directors were happy – but it was a lousy set-up for any player. Every single one of the players was scared stiff of him. He fined me a couple of times and he fined other players, but that wasn't his only weapon. If anyone stepped out of line then they would be made to do extra training. It was a reign of terror he conducted in the dressing-room and there was nothing we could do about it. If you complained then you'd be in for that Sunday session. Or you would be fined. Or you would be dropped. Or you would suffer all three. He didn't care how many times he hit you with punishments, he would just make sure that you hurt.

Bertie Auld would pick on players for the least thing and he could be incredibly vindictive. Once at the end of a morning training session with the full-time players – it was at a period when most of the players were full-time with Thistle – we had a practice game. Auld used to take part in these games which wound up the training, and this time he was playing against me. By chance I stood on his toe. It was an accident, the kind of thing which can happen in any game and does happen in any game. In fact, it happens all the time. It wasn't serious. I stood on his toe and that was that. Except it wasn't over as far as wee Bertie was concerned. He ordered me back to Firhill that afternoon for extra training simply because I had stepped on his toe. I was there running round and round the track while he sat in his office, occasionally coming out to make sure I wasn't slacking. He could do that kind of thing because none of us were able to stand up to him.

He would even keep the players short of tickets for games. The normal thing was that there would be two complimentary tickets available for each player – that was what you would expect. But if Bertie decided otherwise then you would find the ticket allocation for the team cut. I can remember just *fifteen* tickets being distributed amongst all the first-team players for one game. And it was regular that my brother John and I would just get three tickets instead of four because he didn't reckon we needed another one.

He would pick on the craziest things to have a go at you. Pre-match meals were a special time for him to hammer players. He would sit at one of the tables and he would watch everything that every player was eating. Now these meals were usually light – scrambled eggs, omelette, beans on toast for some players – but if he saw a player eating maybe two slices of toast he would go crazy. It was a different world to the one I would eventually find at Liverpool. We would get a meal from the club prior to an away game but on the journey back there would be nothing. And I can remember on one occasion when we were travelling north for a pre-season friendly in the Highlands we stopped at a hotel in Pitlochry for lunch. The waitress came round with menus for all of the players, then Bertie sent the trainer Donnie McKinnon round after her to tell us, "If any of you have the sirloin steak then you have to pay the 30 bob extra yourself." Big-time we weren't!

It was Bertie, too, who tried to move me into midfield again and set my career back for a few months. I had settled into the role at the heart of the defence but Bertie, being Bertie, had other ideas. He pushed me forward into the midfield and by this time I hadn't a clue how to play in that area. Still, there was little point in arguing with Bertie. Once he made up his mind that was that. You questioned his decision at your peril. Of course it wasn't a job sitting in front of the back four he wanted from me – that I could have coped with OK, I'm sure. Nor did he want me playing on the left-hand side of the midfield where I had started off playing when I was at school. No, Bertie had his own ideas. He wanted me on the *right*-hand side of the field. We had little John Craig playing on the left and what Bertie wanted from me was long runs into the opposition's half through the inside-right position. I was supposed to take off on one of these runs whenever John gained possession. Once John had the ball I started the run forward, a long run forward, and he was supposed to try to find me with a crossfield pass. As I said earlier, I was still weak at the time and once I'd made two or three of these runs that was me gone. I couldn't keep it up because I didn't have that kind of stamina. I was quick enough and with full-time training I was getting quicker – but the strength and the extra weight needed had still not arrived.

I went through an unbelievably bad time while Bertie persevered with trying to fit me into this preconceived pattern of play. The tactics were laid down and we had to fit in whether they suited us or not. That didn't concern Bertie all that much. He kept me there for about three months and in that time we had a terrible run in the Premier League until we lost four games on the trot and plunged down towards the relegation zone.

Going into a game against Hearts I read the morning papers on the way in to Firhill and all of them were suggesting that I was going to be axed. There seemed every chance that they were right and I arrived at the ground expecting to be out of the team. Instead he put me back to centre-half and that's where I stayed until I was finally sold. He never once explained why he changed me back, nor did he ever admit he was wrong in playing me in that strange midfield role. Bertie would never do that. In the Hearts game I scored one of the goals and my brother, John, got the other. We won 2-1 and I never looked back.

Bertie came close to destroying me then – and not for the first time. Basically, I'm certain that he kept me there in midfield, even when everyone could see that it was not going to work out, because he was so stubborn. And because he would not admit to making a mistake. The worst I suffered from his stubborn streak, though, was when he made up his mind that I was trying to pull a fast one by claiming I was ill on a day when we were due to play Rangers in a Glasgow Cup game.

The long, rangy stride of Alan Hansen which has become so familiar to the Kop.

At this stage there were only a handful of full-time players with Thistle. Most of the lads were part-timers, having a regular job and training two nights a week at Firhill. The few full-time professionals would train every morning and then also do a stint when all the lads were in at nights. There were maybe half-a-dozen of us who trained as full-timers – Joe Craig, Alan Rough, Benny Rooney, John Craig and myself were definitely there. And even when there was a night game we would go in to Firhill in the morning for a work-out.

This is what happened on the Monday we were due to play this Glasgow Cup match. Except I was ill – and I mean really ill. It had started on the Sunday night and appeared to be a recurrence of a pain I had had several weeks earlier. Then I had had trouble with Bertie because he was always suspicious and always convinced that players were trying to put one over on him. The first time the pain hit me my dad had to call out the doctor because I was in such agony. I had never known anything like it and I haven't experienced anything like it since then either, thank God. The doctor thought it might just be a chill and he ordered me to stay in bed. My dad phoned Firhill and said I was not able to train. The next day Bertie phoned the house and ordered me in to the ground. Once I was there the doctor sent me back home. I stayed in bed, missed the match that week and then seemed to have recovered. But the doctor did warn me that if it struck me again, then it could mean that I would need an appendix operation.

So, here we are on the day we are due to face Rangers and my mate Joe Craig is driving me in to Firhill. Except I'm slumped in the car dying. I am literally doubled up with pain but, again, wee Bertie has ordered me in to the ground so that he can decide whether or not I am fit to train and fit to play in the Glasgow Cup match. I was hardly able to put one foot in front of the other when Joe and I arrived at the ground – but Bertie was adamant. I had to go out and train it off. Whatever was wrong with me would disappear if I went out and worked hard.

That was his answer to most things because deep down he had always convinced himself that players would try to swing the lead when it came to training. He ordered me to put on two track suits and get out on to the ground and start some lapping. I always remember him telling me, "It's the same as you had the other week. It's just a chill and you can sweat it out of you. You'll run it off in a little while."

To begin with he had Joe running round the track with me, then after a few laps he called Joe in and left me out there on my own toiling around on lap after lap and near to collapse. Joe pleaded with him to allow me to stop. Eventually he told Bertie, "He is in big trouble out there. He is really ill. He needs a doctor." Bertie ignored him. Eventually, though, he listened to Joe and did call in the club doctor. But he wouldn't relent. He kept me running round and round the track and I wouldn't stop because I knew what he would do to me if I did – he had this incredible grip on all of us, this fear he held over every single player. It was the doctor who finally told him I had to get off the track. He took one look at me and had me rushed to hospital. That was at midday and I had an appendix operation at four o'clock that afternoon. That's how serious it was.

I can't remember how many laps I ran. It's all a bit of a blank to me now. I seemed to be running – or maybe hobbling is a better word – round and round Firhill in a daze. I can remember it was agonising and I was going round clutching my middle as the pain seared through my stomach. Of course I was kept in hospital for almost a week after that and wee Bertie didn't even come to see me. I don't suppose that should have surprised me but I did think that his conscience might have bothered him just a little bit after what had happened to me. I should have known better.

I suppose it had always been in my mind that I should move on if the chance came, but that kind of treatment made me determined to leave the club. I asked for a transfer and had to suffer Bertie's wrath over that. But I had to let clubs know that I wanted a move and I hoped and hoped that I would get one. There was a spell then when I did not think that anyone was going to come for me and I became pretty downhearted about that. At one time it looked as if Newcastle would come in with a bid but then there was a managerial change there. I think Gordon Lee took over at St James' Park and all the transfer talk came to nothing.

There were rumours, of course, that this club or that club were ready to make Thistle an offer. But there are always rumours going the rounds in football and none of them came to anything. For instance, there were a lot of stories that Celtic were going to buy me. Dave McParland, the man who had signed me for Thistle and the man who had made me a central defender, was at Parkhead as Jock Stein's right-hand man, and so I thought that would happen for me. It was something I could believe because I knew that Dave McParland rated me highly – and it was something I wanted to believe because a move had become important to me. Instead, when Celtic made their move for a Thistle player, it was my mate Joe Craig they signed and I was left behind at Firhill. Then Bolton made an offer and I was sure that this time I would be on my way. But Thistle knocked it back and I was beginning to believe that there was to be no escape from wee Bertie. There was a game at Ibrox around this time, and when we were coming off at the end John Greig, who was then the Rangers captain, shook hands with me and hinted strongly that they were ready to come in – again nothing happened.

I had more or less made up my mind that I was going to be forced to stay with Thistle when Liverpool came in out of the blue. Don't get me wrong – I enjoyed a lot of the time at Thistle. I liked the rest of the players and I enjoyed the Saturday nights after a game when we would all head into the centre of town to the Ivanhoe Hotel to have a few pints together and talk about the game. We were away from Bertie and his reign of terror and it was good and, remember, I was young. Although Thistle didn't pay top money the wages were OK. I was on 50 quid a week and we were on another 20 quid a point in bonus. If we won on a Saturday then I was going out with £90 – it would be nothing today but this was a dozen years ago and it was fine for me. I was able to live comfortably enough on the money I was being paid just to play football. What else could I want? Except, of course, a move to a club where fear didn't rule a player's every move.

Luckily I got that towards the end of the 1976-77 season. It was April when Liverpool offered Thistle £100,000 for my signature and I set off by train to meet the club officials at Anfield.

Hansen is under pressure from an opposing forward here but still looks comfortably in command.

CHAPTER FOUR

Learning the Liverpool Way

ON THAT TRAIN journey south there was never the slightest doubt in my mind that I would take the chance to join Liverpool. It was the kind of move every professional footballer in Britain dreamed about. The men at Anfield were the ultimate in soccer professionals – they were the élite of my chosen profession.

This was my chance of hitting the big time, and if there had been any doubts about just how *big* this club was they would have been rapidly dispelled by the way I was treated when I got to Anfield. The set-up and the offer they made me was impressive – but equally impressive was the way they handled the whole business of the transfer. Thankfully Thistle had not sent Bertie Auld down with me to finalise all the details of the move. Perhaps the directors realised that it would have been a little bit of a nightmare to sit down on a train for several hours with a manager who had almost destroyed my career and who had trained me until I had almost literally dropped. Instead of Bertie, Scot Symon, then general manager of Thistle and the man who had been Rangers' manager for many, many years before that, travelled to Liverpool with me. Over the years Mr

Symon must have been involved in dozens of big-money deals, but even he was surprised by the way Liverpool handled their business. There was a certain style about the way the club secretary Peter Robinson told him that the cheque had been made out and that they would give it to him to take home to Glasgow on the train that night. I can still remember going back north after all the signing formalities had taken place and Mr Symon kept pulling out that cheque for £100,000 and looking at it in awe. He seemed stunned because so many football transfer deals are handled differently. Some clubs like to pay a big transfer fee in instalments and often the other club is happy enough to accept that. Sometimes there can be a delay in the club getting the money together for a massive single payment. But Liverpool had no problems regarding cash and Thistle, struggling financially, had the money for me in their bank account inside 24 hours of my signing.

Too late this time! Alan Hansen desperately tries to block a shot from Manchester United's Lou Macari as Tommy Smith races in behind him. Macari scored.

If they were happy, then I have to admit that I was even happier. On that first contract I signed I was given a basic salary of £150 a week – *three* times what I was getting with Partick Thistle. And my bonuses were considerably more too!

Then we were being paid £125 a point, which gave you £250 for a win bonus – more than six times what I was earning in Scotland.

It wasn't too long before I made the first team . . . and found my whole life had been transformed. I mean, when you have only been with a provincial club in Scotland, then it's a whole new world to suddenly find yourself with the top club in the country. And one of the top clubs in Europe. You are still naïve about things like contracts. To be honest I was just a big, raw laddie when I made the move south. Even going home on the train I was a little apprehensive because I had signed a blank contract. The club had told me what the salary would be and I had accepted that as gospel and signed. Then I began to wonder if I had done the right thing – of course, I had. And down through the years with Liverpool I've learned that when the club says something, or when they promise you something, then you get it. That was my first lesson in learning trust, and from that time on I have never felt let down by this club or by the men who have run it.

The other thing which hit me was that there was all this money being paid into my bank in Alloa during the summer months of the close season while I was still at home. I couldn't quite believe all of that. At Firhill your 50 quid was cut back in the summer and you were given close season wages only. I hadn't even thought to ask Liverpool if there was any difference in the wages when the close season arrived. Of course that didn't happen with big-time outfits – but I hadn't known that. It took me some time to come to terms with this new wealth. It was nice to know that you were suddenly making so much more money than you had ever been able to earn before – and yet it was also a bit disconcerting because I had not expected it. And I certainly wasn't used to it.

The way the players were treated was also very different to my experiences. When I first signed I went back down and stayed for a week at the Holiday Inn while I found my feet. The first night there I took a look at the prices on the restaurant menu and I hardly ordered a thing. I was scared to have a meal there because it seemed so expensive. For the first day or two I was living on snacks which were sent up to my room – I didn't dare order too much in case I couldn't afford to pay the bill at the end of the week. Then I learned one day at training that I had nothing to worry about – the club footed the bill. I thought back to Pitlochry and that lunch stop with Thistle when we were told we would have to pay extra ourselves if we wanted a steak. I realised this was my brave new world . . ..

I soon learned that every little thing about Liverpool Football Club, every little detail, has been looked after. Nothing is ever left to chance and the players are treated as the most important members of the club. There seems to be a fairly straightforward and simple philosophy about the whole Anfield set-up – if someone is doing a good job for the club then he is rewarded for that. If someone steps out of line, or lets the club down on the field, then he will be dropped. And maybe even sold. Above all they are a loyal club, loyal to their players, and that breeds loyalty from the players to the club.

I told you about the first contract I signed, but the later ones I agreed to with the club illustrate even more the way they create trust inside the dressing-room. For example, I have never once asked Liverpool Football Club for a rise. I have never felt the need to go in to see Peter Robinson or any of the managers and demand an increase – for the simple reason that I have never felt let down by the club financially. They have looked after me all through my career.

After I had been at Anfield for a year I had more or less established myself in the first team. I had played in the European Cup final against Bruges and they called me in that summer and told me simply that they had doubled my wages. I didn't have to say a word to anyone. I was called in, told I had done well for the club and that my salary had been doubled. No fuss. No hassle. Just done in that simple straightforward way that has become the club's hallmark. The following year I had played for Scotland and this time Bob Paisley had me in to his office and told me I would be on the same bonus as every other international player at the club. They work a system whereby if you are playing for your country, or have played for your country, then you automatically qualify for extra money from the club. Once again, I didn't have to ask for this – it arrived. Since then I have signed, I think, three contracts with the club, and all of them have been settled inside five minutes. I've gone in with a salary figure in mind, and I've usually found that they have had a figure very close to mine under consideration. On each occasion they have been able to offer me more or less exactly what I had hoped for. I haven't had the slightest problem with contracts. You hear about players having problems at other clubs – but I have never had the slightest complaint about how the financial side of my career has been handled by Liverpool.

OK, you can take a look at the club's balance sheet and you might see that there are a couple of players who are earning more money than the others. Over the years these players could have been Rushie and Kenny Dalglish or maybe Graeme Souness before he left the club to play in Italy with Sampdoria. I don't know exactly who they were and it really doesn't concern me overmuch either. The way I see it is simple – some players probably deserve to be paid more than others. You always get players who are bigger names, bigger stars, if you like, than others, and maybe there are players who do get upset about that. I don't. I have always felt the same way about things. If you go in to discuss a new contract and you come out happy with the deal which has been laid out in front of you, then you have nothing to complain about. You should be content to stick by that without worrying about the deals which other players have been able to negotiate for themselves.

I don't see there is anything to be gained by taking a look at what someone else is earning and then going about complaining. I've maybe been lucky but I have always been happy with the contracts which have been offered to me. I've never felt that I should be getting this or that simply because someone else has been lucky enough to get it. That's not in my make-up. In any case, I tend to take the view that if you are not too greedy, too demanding, then there are other ways a club can

Hansen's mate Terry McDermott holding the FA Charity Shield after a Wembley win.

look after you. Certainly, in my own case, Liverpool have looked after me well in the years I have spent with them. Quite apart from granting me a testimonial year which was very successful financially for me, I cannot think of a single complaint I could level at the club. All that time and nothing has caused me the slightest bit of unhappiness.

Basically, Anfield is a good place to be – a good place to play your football, a good place to follow a career in the game, and somehow, during the years I've been there, Liverpool have been able to keep almost all in the player pool happy. I don't know how they have done that exactly, because if you are out of the first team then life can be pretty miserable. That applies anywhere in the world and with any club. At Liverpool the managers have always maintained that every single player in the first-team squad of around 18 is equally important. They insist that even those not playing are still vital to the club and still a part of the club's thrust towards titles and trophies.

That's all right for a manager to say – but it's not always all right for the players. Once you drop out of the team then you seem to be moping around the place because you really want to be involved in playing week after week. There is nothing worse than training for four or five days and then, at the end of it all, finding out that you are sitting in a seat in the stand while the other lads are playing. Maybe it's the fact that there is good money paid at Liverpool to everyone who makes up the squad, and that can keep players content to hang on there as reserves when they could be playing in the first team at almost any other club in the First Division. Then again maybe it's just that there is such a good atmosphere and a strong feeling of loyalty among the players that helps keep everyone more or less happy. Whatever the secret is I'd like to know it – just as every manager in Britain would like to know it. Because the job of keeping top-class players happy when they are out of the first team must be the hardest part of all for a manager.

The strength of the club is probably in the dressing-room. It is there that you are taught to mix well with the other lads. It's there that this feeling of comradeship is built up. So much so that I can remember Michael Robinson coming back for a few days' holiday from Spain, where he was playing for Real Osasuna, and telling me that he would rather be playing with Liverpool reserves than with any other club. He was almost in tears the day he left Anfield, even though he knew that he was going to be playing first-team football regularly in the Spanish First Division and that he had been well looked after financially. That mattered because he had to look to his future – but the wrench at leaving was still great.

You see, whenever a player arrives at Anfield then he is literally forced to mix well and become a part of the squad. The atmosphere in the dressing-room is superb and off the field there is the same kind of kinship. That has always been the way of the club in the dozen years that I have been there. There is always someone who can come to the club and is a little bit of a loner. Or who may be a bit of a big-head. But if they behave in that way in the dressing-room the lads simply destroy them. Not in a nasty way, really, but in that wind-up way that footballers have. Eventually everyone becomes a part of the group and it's in that camaraderie that the spirit of the team flourishes.

Don't ask me how that started with the club, probably it stems from the days when Bill Shankly was the manager and Bob Paisley was his assistant. It seems always to have been a part of the Liverpool mystique. It has been there as long as I've been at the club, but I don't think it has ever been as strong and powerful a force as it is today. It was always good but there wasn't as much mixing with the lads off the field as there is today. And as there was in the years soon after I moved into the first-team squad. Phil Thompson and Terry McDermott were the senior professionals who looked after me most of all when I first went down. They kind of took me under their wings and made sure that I was not going to be too much on my own and that there would be no way that I would get homesick. I always appreciated what they did for me in those early days because the mixing together socially wasn't anything as strong as it has since become.

The great thing was that there were very few rucks in the dressing-room when someone was dropped and another player was moved into his position. I suppose the all-pervading professionalism made sure of that. Players knew what was expected from them and they knew that with 16 or 18 players around, then there was always the chance of having to drop out of the team at some stage or another. There would be a bit of chat in the dressing-room during the week when it looked as if there was going to be a change. A bit of banter, a few choice words. But when the team was announced then that was that. No cribs. No public disagreements. As the managers have said repeatedly, the club has to be put first by all the lads.

To go back for a moment to the squad system, I've always felt that it's good for the club, good for the manager, good for the 11 players who are in the team, but, basically, lousy for the half-dozen or so who cannot get a place. I've never fully accepted the argument that the game today is a squad game. As a player I think you are either in the team and playing, or you are out of the team and not playing. That for any player is surely the beginning and end of any story. It's only natural that you won't be happy playing in the reserves in front of a few hundred people when you have been used to First Division games in front of huge crowds. And it's even worse for most of us when you are asked to sit in the stand as a spectator after you have worked and trained all week hoping that you might be in the side.

I think the pain of being more or less a permanent squad player, as opposed to a first-team player, was eased for the lads when we had European successes. They felt more a part of all of that because they were more involved when five substitutes could be used. Now, because that has been missing from our season ever since the dreadful disaster at the Heysel Stadium, I believe it has probably been more difficult for Kenny Dalglish to keep the players happy all the time. How he has done it is a miracle.

But going back to the days when we were in Europe, players knew that if they were in the pool of 16 players then they had a

Alan Hansen's defensive partner on so many occasions, Phil Thompson, in First Division action for Liverpool.

chance to taste the European action – maybe even pick up a
European Cup medal at the end of a season – and so everyone
could feel a part of the club's success. It was almost essential to
have that kind of incentive for the players who were being left
out of the first team regularly, as the chances of getting into the
League side could be fairly remote. You would have to sit and
wait for someone to be injured; or suspended; or to lose form
dramatically – and that didn't happen too often. If you did get
into the team and you happened to be replacing Kenny
Dalglish or Graeme Souness, then your promotion would be
strictly temporary. These two along with Ray Clemence were
the untouchables as far as team selection was concerned. They
were the élite group which there always seemed to be at the
club – the players who might be forced to drop out for one
reason or another but who would be straight back in when they
became available once more. I can never recall there being
more than three or four of them in the team at any one time. As
for the rest of us, if we went out then we just had to take our
chances of fighting back at times. Apart from the tiny group I
mentioned, no one was encouraged to take it for granted that
they would simply stroll back into the League side whenever
their injury had cleared or their suspension was over.

I can remember being brought back myself after being
injured in 1982. I had damaged my knee and missed the Milk
Cup final against Spurs. I was out for that and for maybe six
First Division games. The team won the Cup without me, won
all these games too, and went to the top of the table. For some
reason, though, they wanted me back in the side – even though
I'd never seen myself as one of those players who wouldn't be
left on the sidelines if it suited the backroom staff. They had
had me working hard with the reserves – in midfield too. Back
to the days of Firhill and wee Bertie. But they only wanted me
in there to test the strength of my leg and to see how it would
stand up under the strain of long runs. Anyhow, that Tuesday
night I played at Huddersfield in the reserves and the next
morning Joe Fagan, who was assistant to Bob Paisley then,
came up to me at training to ask if I thought I was fit again. I

said I was fine, even though that single reserve game didn't seem enough of a test after being out for so long. At any rate, that night the first team went to Old Trafford and won 1-0.

In the meantime I had gone home from training before going through to Manchester to watch the game. While at home I somehow managed to drop a glass in the kitchen. It bounced off a worktop and then smashed into my right leg. I felt it go into the leg but, at the time, I didn't realise that it might be serious. Then, suddenly there was blood seeping through my trousers and I knew that I had to get something done quickly. I went to hospital, where they were forced to stitch a gash which ran across my right knee. I had to have half-a-dozen stitches put in the wound. Because of the stitches I could not train on the Thursday morning. No one from the backroom staff came near me. Joe ignored me, so did Ronnie Moran, and I was left on my own walking around the training-ground worrying about the gash in my leg. I can remember thinking, "They might at least come up and ask me how my knee is". But they didn't. They just left me to my own devices.

Then on Friday when I was working out, back came Joe to ask me, "Do you fancy playing tomorrow?" Just like that. Out of the blue. And what was I supposed to answer to that one? I could not really believe that this was happening. The team had to go back to Manchester to meet City at Maine Road – another tough, tough game. And yet even though they had been going so well and even though they had won at Old Trafford, they wanted me back in the side. I'd had the one solitary reserve game. Now I'd had six stitches in my knee and they wanted to know if I was ready. Of course, in these circumstances there is just no way at all that you can say, "No, I don't really fancy playing in the first team yet." To do that might finish your career at Liverpool. I wasn't exactly ecstatic about the thought of going in so soon after missing all of these games and not being able to do all the training that I would have liked to. But I could only say "Yes" and then wait to see how they handled it from there. It was their little bit of psychology, you see. They left me brooding on Thursday and then lifted me on the Friday. It's the kind of thing they do all the time, and even though you know what they are up to, it still works so very well. Maybe I wasn't certain that the leg would stand up to 90 minutes in the First Division but I wasn't going to say that – I was going to go out to prove that I was OK, that I deserved to be back in the team. They knew that all right!

Of course, everyone thought that the man who would be dropping out of the team would be Phil Thompson, but again the backroom boys had a surprise up their sleeves. Tommo played and I played and it was my mate Terry McDermott who was axed. I had told the lads that I was being sounded out about a recall and there were a few choice words in the dressing-room about things because we all knew that someone was going to have to face up to being dropped – never the easiest thing to accept, especially if the team has been on a good run as Liverpool had been at that particular time. Anyway, it was Terry Mac's turn and he wasn't happy about it. However, he knew like all of us that this was what life was like at a big club. Even though Terry was looked on as one of the most influential players at Anfield then, it didn't matter. He was out and I was in – and I still cannot tell you the reasoning behind that one. Luckily my knee held up and we won again and I stayed in the team until the end of the season.

It's a funny thing about Liverpool – they changed my whole outlook on the game. If I had gone to any other club I would never have known the success I have had here at Anfield. That goes without saying. But I would also have been less of a player, less of a professional than I have become, because it was Liverpool who turned me into a real pro. And it was Liverpool who transformed me into a winner. They teach you that second best is not enough and so, here was I, someone who didn't even start off a football career for the right reasons, being told what was expected of me at the hardest, most demanding school in soccer. I had more or less drifted into the game to escape a lifetime in insurance offices. And the casual attitude which was so difficult for me to shake off stayed with me until Liverpool's backroom staff taught me differently. They turned me into a

A man of the match award brought Alan Hansen an autographed cue and case from snooker ace Steve Davis.

Hansen tries his hand at another ball game but snooker king Steve Davis is less than impressed by his efforts.

winner. The Anfield Academy taught me about winning and just how much it can mean to you. I could have gone elsewhere and been happy enough just playing away and picking up nice money at the end of the week. Bob Paisley and Joe Fagan and Ronnie Moran and the lads in the team when I first broke through showed me there was more to life than that. Once you get a taste of winning, once you get the smell of greasepaint and hear the roar of the crowd, and once you pick up your first winner's medal, then you're hooked. Liverpool made me a winner. Probably no other club would have been able to do that. That's why I have never wanted to play anywhere else but at Anfield. Nowhere else can match this place.

CHAPTER FIVE

"Jock Pictures" at Anfield

IT IS INCREDIBLE to look back on the really great years I
have had at Liverpool and realise what the club has achieved in
that time. During my years in the first team we have won the
First Division championship seven times, the FA Cup once
and the League Cup four times. We have also collected three
European Cup victories and in one season we took the League
and Cup double at home. It's something I never, ever thought I
would be lucky enough to be a part of. All these glittering prizes
seemed away beyond me, well out of reach of someone
plodding away for Partick Thistle.

Yet it has all happened and it has been particularly good that
I could share so much of it with my mates. I've said elsewhere
that almost all of the lads were close off the field, but I suppose
Kenny and Graeme and myself were closest of all. We stuck
together a little because we were the Jocks in the dressing-room
and we would have to take a bit of stick about that from the
other lads. We also enjoyed dishing it out when we had the
chance to do so.

One of the standing jokes at Anfield for us was when we won
a Cup or when the League Championship trophy had been

The Three Musketeers of Anfield – or 'Three Jocks', Dalglish, now Liverpool manager, Hansen, now Liverpool captain, and Souness, now boss of Rangers.

presented, the three of us would try to get hold of it and have a special "Jock" picture taken by one of our photographer mates from Southport, Harry Ormesher. We would get hold of it and the shout would go up – "Jock pictures, Jock pictures". The other lads would be cracking up because we wouldn't let them into the photograph until the three of us had been taken. Even Terry Mac, my pal, or Ray Clemence, who taught me so much about the game, or Phil Thompson, who was another mate, could not get into those pictures. It was done just for the three of us and the pictures became a little bit special for us.

It started by accident, at the first of our European Cup wins – the first of those we shared in, that is – at Wembley in 1978 when Harry O snapped a picture of us as we congratulated each other. We had a few years of that, a few years when we would have these pictures taken and kid the hell out of the English lads. Then it stopped. When it was getting to the stage that there were too many Scots to fit into the Jock pictures we called a halt. By the time Stevie Nicol and Gary Gillespie were in the side that time was over. But those are still pictures I treasure and I like to think that Kenny and Graeme feel the same way.

Many people in Scotland won't believe all of this because they don't want to believe that players in England care as passionately for their country as the lads at home do. You always get the cry for an all-Scottish team, or, I should say, an all-Tartan team, one that would leave the Anglos sitting on the sidelines. It's all so much nonsense because in those days at Liverpool there were times when I felt more Scottish than I did when I was at Firhill. If Scotland won at anything the three of us used to go crazy in the dressing-room, winding up the other lads about it. I mean, if it was the world tiddlywinks championship or something equally daft then we would boast about it. It used to get up the noses of the English lads, I suppose, but it was all a part of the dressing-room wind-ups.

The sad thing was that no one back home could see what went on behind the scenes and so Kenny and Graeme would go back to play at Hampden for Scotland and end up getting stick. I've said elsewhere how that happened to me before one game

King Kenny, master of all he surveys.

there, but it happened to them more than that. Yet when they were fit they went up there to play despite the hostility which was sometimes shown to them.

I've known both sides of the issue because I played in Scotland – as Kenny did – but Graeme went south as a kid. He was with Spurs when he was just 15 years old and so he spent most of his life in England. Certainly the best part of his career was south of the Border with that extra bonus of two years in Italy before he returned to Rangers. And it must have been hard for him to accept and harder for him to understand.

Being called an 'Anglo' hurt in itself – although I have to admit to having some kind of resentment against the English-based players myself when I was with Thistle. And Graeme, later to become my mate, was one of the targets of that jealousy. When I was picked for an under-21 team while I was at Firhill I was never too crazy about some of the players who came from the bigger English clubs.

I can remember one occasion in particular when I thought Graeme was a really flash kind of person and I could never imagine being friends with him at all. Don't ask me to explain it – and I know now how wrong that feeling was because I've suffered myself – but it was there. Maybe it was because we all knew that they earned loadsamoney. Maybe it was because they wore better gear. But whatever it was I remember going to Sweden with the under-21 team and Graeme was there too with the full international side. The two teams travelled together and stayed together because both games against Sweden were on the same day but at different times and in different stadiums. Anyhow Graeme was cutting about with Ted McDougall on that particular trip and I can still remember thinking to myself, "They fancy their chances a bit, don't they". Here I was on one of my first international trips and I was thinking that way. It was daft but it happened and eventually I was to find out how far that image was from the truth. I mean, I never really got to know Ted McDougall but at Liverpool I came to know Graeme really well. And the impression I had on that trip to Gothenburg was totally and utterly wrong.

Graeme Souness and Kenny Dalglish – two who played so often for Scotland while Hansen sat out of the international games.

One of the "Jock pictures" – with Alan Hansen and Kenny Dalglish and Graeme Souness celebrating yet another trophy victory.

OK, Graeme does have the image of being 'flash', and we can all remember Bob Paisley's remark that when he made Graeme his captain he expected him to toss up before the start of games with an American Express Gold Card. He dresses well. He wears expensive clothes, expensive watches and drives a big car. But at heart he is just a basic, out-and-out Jock. One of the first things he used to do when we got home to join the Scotland squad was to get himself a fish supper. Yet the fans seemed to resent him. When he was getting all that stick from the fans at Hampden I used to wind him up a little – in fact, if I was in the team and on the field for the warm-up I used to keep hitting the ball to him to make sure he was always in possession, because every time he touched it he would get the bird. We used to really get him at it. Obviously he knew what I was up to, and I used to kid him as we were going down the tunnel. I know that deep down it hurt him – and I know that Jock Stein used to feel for him when that happened. He used to get more abuse from the Scottish fans than the opposing players got. It was incredible and terribly unfair.

I had to admire the way Graeme took that for so long. Game

after game he would get it no matter how well he played. I would have understood if he had opted out. I'm sure managers like Jock Stein would have understood if he had said, "I've had enough". But it was never Graeme's way to quit. He was always one to face up to things. We all knew that at Liverpool. He would never walk away when he was in trouble – he would battle his way through things.

The people who really know Graeme Souness are the people who have been with him when the going has got tough. At Liverpool he was liked and respected by all the lads. We knew that if anyone was in trouble then Graeme would be there to help him out. That was the way he was – and I'm sure that the Rangers lads have found the same. He would never hide from anything. If someone had to take responsibility then he would be the first volunteer. That's the way I have always seen Graeme, and I just wish that the Scottish supporters had been able to see him the same way as his playing colleagues did.

Guess who? It's the Anfield Christmas party again with the three Scots – pirate Alan Hansen, Kenny Dalglish as Russ Abbott's Scotsman and Steve Nicol blacked up.

None of us ever had any doubts about Graeme Souness or his commitment to whatever cause he was playing for. At club level with Liverpool and at international level with Scotland. Graeme was the perfect professional and the perfect example for any player.

So was Kenny Dalglish. We were lucky to have the two of them available at the same time. And yet even Kenny was a victim of the Hampden boo boys for a long spell in his career. I think he had it before Graeme began to catch it and then it moved on to me – Nicol had better be careful or he'll be next!

In Kenny's case I can remember one day when we played Argentina at Hampden. It was the year after they had won the World Cup and Maradona was just making his breakthrough. We lost 3-1. That afternoon Kenny was the target for the jeers. He suffered really badly. From the start of that game the fans were on his back. Every time he touched the ball he was booed and, of course, Kenny, being the kind of person he is, simply tried harder and harder. It was sad to be there and see the torment he went through. In fact, it was even worse to be on the field with him because we all suffered with Kenny that day. Then, soon afterwards, things changed for him. By the end of his career he was like a god to the fans, and that was the way it should always have been. Not too many players have a record as good as Kenny's. He played in three World Cups – in West Germany in 1974, in Argentina in 1978 and in Spain in 1982 – and he could have been in a fourth in Mexico except for an injury ruling him out at the last minute. He also collected more than 100 caps – the only Scottish player ever to achieve that target. It was just good that by the end the fans realised just what a giant of a player Kenny Dalglish was. Eventually he could do nothing wrong in their eyes, and it was good to see that.

Mind you, it wasn't a problem which was unique to our period in the Scottish team. Before our time Denis Law had suffered the same, and he also ended up a hero. I hope that kind of barracking has ended now. As I say, I suffered myself from some of the resentment to the Anglos that the fans so obviously

Kenny Dalgish won every honour as a player – being a manager hasn't changed anything. Here he is with the Manager of the Year trophy.

felt. It's a strange thing to look back and see that you were affected in the same way supporters were – stranger when you become a victim of the anti-Anglo feelings!

You do try to joke about it, mainly because that is the one way you can perhaps handle the emotional pain which strikes you. The last time it happened to me was when I went up to Pittodrie to play in a testimonial match for John McMaster. Probably that came because there was a rivalry between Willie Miller and myself for the Scotland role as 'sweeper', and this was not too long before the Mexico World Cup finals. If the fans had known I was going to be left at home they might have saved their boos for someone else – but they didn't and I was the guy getting it hot and strong. Before the game had started the fans in one section of the crowd had slaughtered me. Stevie Nicol came racing over towards me, just as I used to do with Graeme. He warmed up alongside me and gave me a few verbals of his own. That kept me going when my head might have gone down. Laughing to keep from crying is what you might call it.

The most important thing, though, was that the kind of stick we got didn't make us any less eager to play for our country. The hurt persisted at times, but we knew that we wanted to play for Scotland. We knew that playing our football and earning our living in England didn't make us any less Scottish. Indeed, we knew that because we were exiles we became even more Scottish than some people who stay at home.

Most of all, though, Kenny and Graeme and I had the Jock pictures to sustain us when times got bad. They spoke for us. They told the world how we felt. Just as proud of being Scottish as we were of being in that great, great Liverpool side.

CHAPTER SIX

Bob and Joe and Kenny and Graeme

OUTSIDE OF LIVERPOOL the major influence on my career was my father. He had played as a junior with a local team called Camelon and had once participated in the Scottish Junior Cup final at Hampden in front of 72,000 people. I never achieved that until I played in the European Cup final at Wembley against Bruges and he used to remind me of that – often!

But he also made me toe the line when I was a youngster. I could be a little bit rebellious and he made sure that I did train and that I did turn up for the different teams I played for. He also tried to guide me towards the right kind of club. He had faith in me. It was always my father who thought that I would make it as a player and I owe him a great deal for that. However, once you leave home, and once you are playing professionally, then the managers you play under dominate your life. They are the ones who can make or break you. The men who can set up a career for a player or end it. There is a certain ruthlessness about the best of managers and I don't see how that could be any other way. Their job is to make sure that their club is successful. If one player or two players or even more have to be sacrificed for the good of the club – and for the good of the majority of the players – then that's what has to happen. All of us in the game know that.

It's been interesting to look at the managers closely and to see how the three bosses I've had at Liverpool have handled the job. I've also stolen a look at my old pal Graeme Souness. I know Graeme so well from our years together at Anfield that, although I'm viewing his managerial role from a distance, I'm sure I know what makes him tick!

Bob Paisley, of course, was the man who signed me. Even if he had done no more than that I would have been eternally grateful to him because he gave me the opportunity of playing with the best team in Britain. And, for long enough, the best team in Europe too. While other managers dithered about, wondering whether they should take a chance on me – this too slow, too casual, too weak central defender with Partick Thistle – Bob Paisley moved in quickly and made me a Liverpool player. He had a lot of faith in me and I just hope I repaid all of it for him.

When Bob appeared on television the public saw this guy with the wide grin on his face and that quaint Geordie accent which I could never really understand. He was like everyone's favourite uncle. Everybody liked him. He never seemed to get himself involved in rows with referees or other managers – certainly not in public. But there was a completely ruthless streak in Bob. Without any shadow of doubt Bob Paisley was totally ruthless when it came to looking after Liverpool Football Club. He had a basic philosophy about management which appeared to be rooted in personal experience – one which clearly hurt him deeply at the time. He would always go on about this incident in his own playing career when he was in the Liverpool side all the way up to the English Cup final at Wembley in 1949 – and then he was dropped. Just like that, he was left out of the team for the biggest game in English football. When he became team boss after Bill Shankly he always maintained that that experience of his own stood him in good stead when it came to making decisions about the team. If he decided that a player had to be axed then that was that. Sentiment did not come into it. The player might have been playing – as he had done himself – all through the season and he could be expecting to play in a big glamour game at the end. But if he was not the right choice for the team then he would be out. And Bob would not lose any sleep over it. He was right, too. If a manager does show any sign of sentiment then that can quickly become a weakness, and once that happens a team can begin to fail.

Bob Paisley – a "completely ruthless manager", says Hansen.

Bob knew all of that. He had been with the club for so long and in the game for so long, and he recognised the one sure way to failure was to allow any kind of sentiment to interfere with the job. No manager can afford that. Bob, though, was the master of it. In all the time I played under him I never saw him lose an argument. If he made up his mind on something then that was it. No one could budge him. He knew that he had to stand or fall by his own decisions and he was prepared to do that. But he knew, as well, that he had to be right, and so to make sure that he was right he remained utterly ruthless in the way he handled players. It was that streak in him which made him such a magnificent manager and which helped make Liverpool the great club they are. He would have his *best* team fixed in his mind and that would be the team he would stand or fall by unless injury intervened.

Bob wasn't great on chopping and changing. He wanted consistency in performance from the players and gave them back consistency in the team for as long as he could. One of the seasons when we won the Championship Bob managed to do that using only 12 players! It was quite incredible. We just went on and on with scarcely an injury and Bob was able to play what he believed to be his best team for game after game until the title was taken. He had an economy about his team selections if injuries were avoided.

Then, if injuries did disturb the team, Bob would push someone in and invariably, no matter how well that player might be doing, he would be out again if Bob wanted to get back to his "settled side". It wouldn't matter to Bob if the player had scored a hat-trick in the previous game, or been magnificent in defence, or whatever. If Bob decided he was *out* then that was it. And who could argue with him? The man's record proved that he was almost always right and I'm sure that Bob never lost a wink of sleep about the often cruel decisions he had to make. Some of them must have come close to wrecking players' careers but if it was the right decision for Liverpool then Bob used the axe mercilessly.

He could also blow his top in the dressing-room and that was a sight to see. I can remember one occasion in particular when Alan Kennedy was the victim – not because he had played badly and not because we had just lost an Easter Monday game 3-1 to Aston Villa at Villa Park. No, Alan's crime had been to predict that we had won the Championship already because we had gone to Old Trafford and beaten Manchester United 2-0 on the Saturday. The newspaper headlines were screaming out Alan's message as we travelled to Birmingham: "We are the

champions: Kennedy" and various other messages saying more
or less the same. Well, after the game Bob came in and went
crazy. I thought he was going to have a heart attack. His hair
was all over the place, he could hardly get his words out and he
was spluttering and shouting. All of the fury was directed at
Alan. Now, this was the season we won the title and lost just 16
goals in doing so, but because someone had dared to shout
about what we might do Bob was raging. He hated that. All of
the managers have hated that. They reckoned that should be
left to other clubs. The view from the boot room at Anfield was
simple: "Let the others do the shouting off the field, we'll do
our bit on the field." If anyone ever doubted how much they
meant that, then that day at Villa taught them a lesson. The
thing to do at Anfield is to keep your mouth shut until you have
achieved something. Don't tempt the fates beforehand. Alan
Kennedy found that out the hardest way of all – by having to
face one of Bob's tirades.

*Power is handed over – significantly enough in the Anfield boot room. This is
the moment when Bob Paisley handed over managerial duties to Joe Fagan.*

Bob never did like players boasting about what they might do, or beginning to believe that they were better than he thought they were. He reckoned that once a team began to listen to newspaper talk about how great they all were, then problems would set in. He would say: "If players start believing in all the publicity surrounding them, then you have the start of trouble in the team. Not one team has 11 great players – you are lucky if you have one or two who can be classed great. Once you get 11 believing that, then you have problems. When the other nine players in the team reckon they are also entitled to be called great, then look out." We were never encouraged to think that. Bob and the rest of the backroom staff would go out of their way to bring you down to earth if they thought you were getting carried away. And, of course, the other players in the dressing-room did their share of that as well. No one was allowed to get too big-headed. At the first sign of that you could expect a volley from the lads and a follow-up from the training staff. You learn quickly that you get nothing for talking a good game.

You can only win respect at Anfield by going out there and doing it. That's what they respect more than anything else. Bob has always preached that, and if there is an Anfield secret then that is it. They don't have time for any "dodgepots". They won't tolerate the guys who operate in the games they fancy and then are marked absent in others. What Bob liked above all were the players who performed all the time, week in and week out, and who still did the business even when they didn't fancy it.

Terry Mac and myself were non-fanciers. He used to sit beside me in the dressing-room and say, "I wish it was five o'clock and I had a pint of lager in my hand." In my early days I maybe didn't fancy going out there and doing it nine times out of ten, but I would get out and probably I'd perform well enough in four or five out of the ten. As I got tougher mentally under the guidance of Bob and Joe and Ronnie, then I might not fancy many more games but I'd be able to do the business in seven or eight of them. Liverpool used to set great store by that. It's impossible to have the attitude that you want to get out on the field in every game out of the 80 or more you might play in a season. There are times when you don't feel 100 per cent fit, when you just reckon the demands are becoming too much. You had to push that aside. And when you looked around the dressing-room you could see the archetypal Liverpool players in Graeme and Kenny, who would go out there and do it every time. Maybe there were times when they didn't play well, but they would be in there pitching for the team – until the death. The grooming you got at Liverpool made you do that.

It was probably a natural progression that when Bob Paisley stepped aside, Joe Fagan should step up and take his place as the new manager. It was the way it had happened all those years earlier when Bill Shankly went. Then Bob was the man promoted from the boot room to make sure that the standards set at the club would be maintained and the emphasis would be placed on the same values. On the training-ground; on the field; and off the field, as well. Joe had been there with Bob and Shanks and it was a continuation of things that were right for Liverpool . . . almost a boot-room dynasty, if you like.

It isn't always easy to step up from being coach to being manager. It's a hard school, football, and not everyone can bridge the gap. But Bob had done it and put his own stamp on the team and Joe was able to do it too. He was 62 years old when he was named as the club manager and he had been steeped in the ways of Anfield for 26 years. In his first full season in charge of the team Joe guided us to victories in the Milk Cup and the League Championship and also brought the club the European Cup for the fourth time.

It was a fantastic record for the man and yet he always seemed to be downgraded a little by people outside the club. They tended to talk about how Joe had inherited a good team from Bob Paisley. But what those people tend to forget is that this is only half the battle. You can have good players – but it's not always that you can get them to play for you. I think we have all seen cases, at other clubs, when a new manager is appointed and he has good players but things don't work out. The new man still has to run the side. And he has to impose his own personality on the side, although in Joe's case that wasn't essential because part of his personality was with us already after all those years he had been working with the players. He was a man who was greatly respected by all the players and I like to think that all of us went out of our way to try to do well for him.

Joe achieved results in a slightly different way from Bob. He was not nearly as ruthless, for instance. His approach was the "arm round the shoulder" one. He would come up to you at training and pull you to one side and then drop in a quiet word of advice here and there about how you were playing. He was famous for that "word in the ear" routine. Even before he was manager that was one of his trademarks. It was always typical Liverpool words of wisdom he would hand to the players, too.

The "backroom boys" at Anfield have always been great for keeping players slightly on edge – at least that's my construction on how they handle that off-field advice. You can be going through a lousy spell and one of them will take you aside – it used to be Joe, of course – and tell you just how marvellously you are doing. "Just keep it up," he would say and then walk off and leave you wondering. Then, if you are playing well, or *you* think that you are playing well, they will bring you down to earth by telling you that your performances have been rubbish. It's like a little game that they play but it has a serious end product. They study players and watch for little signs that will tell them whether you need a word of encouragement or a word which will stop you becoming too satisfied with the way you have been playing. The funny thing is you recognise what they are up to – or what you think they are up to – but it still works. If they give you a little boost then you can feel lifted by that for the next game. Or if they slag you off then you feel that you have to prove something to them. It's their psychology and Joe was the man who put his arm around your shoulders and dropped the words of wisdom in your ear.

As long as I knew Joe he was the one who put that word in your ear at the right time. I always felt that Joe was uncomfortable about having to drop players. Unlike Bob, who would axe anyone when he thought the team needed it, Joe didn't like that. Nor did he seem happy about the trappings of the job. He always seemed to be happier in the boot room than he was in the manager's office. The manager's job is essentially different from that of a coach and Joe liked the camaraderie of the boot room. So many things were discussed there, decided there, dissected there, down through the years, that I doubt if he ever wanted to be cut off from that essential side of Anfield life. I mean, that boot room became a bit of a legend. Not only at Anfield but right through the game. It was where visiting managers would be after a game and people such as Jock Stein, when he was Scotland manager, loved to go in there and sit around and hear the stories that were being told and the post-mortems which were taking place. Joe had been there for so long that maybe he found it hard to cut a part of himself off from that.

The backroom boys – Joe Fagan with coach Ronnie Moran, two of the men who guided Liverpool to so much greatness.

He still goes there, even though he has been away from the club for three years and more. You can sometimes catch him heading for there after a game when you are coming out of the dressing-room. He will be there to talk and listen and to reminisce. I don't know what exactly they talk about in there but it's a fair bet that 99 per cent of the conversation is about football. And Liverpool's football, in particular.

I honestly believed that Joe made the transition well from there to the manager's office, and like everyone else about the place I was shattered when he decided to call it a day. Never for a moment did I think he would go. Things had not gone as well as they had done in his first year – but they had not gone badly either. We were second in the First Division. We were runners-up in the European Cup – though the grey shadow of the Heysel Stadium hung over the result. And we had managed to do that despite losing Graeme Souness to Italian football. Graeme had been one of the most influential players in the team. He was close to being irreplaceable and all of us realised that. Which is why the results in the second season under Joe's leadership didn't strike us as being disastrous.

The funny thing was that there was no little sniff in the dressing-room about possible changes. Usually there is something, just a little thing here and there which lets you sense that things are going to be changing. This time there was nothing. Not one of us had any inkling that Joe was to retire. It was hard to believe. One day he was there. The next he had gone, and I don't think any of us could properly work out the reasons for it. Perhaps, as I suspected, he didn't fully enjoy the change of role inside the club. But, more to the point, he probably did not enjoy the publicity which was thrust upon him as manager of Liverpool. Joe had always been happy as a background figure at the club. He enjoyed that. I don't know if he cared too much for the press conferences he had to give and the television interviews that are so much part and parcel of the manager's life. Joe was the type of man who would enjoy the essentials of the job – but not the public side of it. He would enjoy working with players and pitting his wits against the

The worries of management are etched deep in Joe Fagan's face. Hansen believes the non-football side of the job wasn't to Fagan's liking.

opposing managers. He would enjoy proving himself as a manager after the years in the shadows. But being hauled clear of these shadows and pushed into the limelight wasn't maybe the thing for him. That may have had something to do with his leaving. Or maybe he just felt that it was time for him to step aside and allow a younger man the chance to take over. I don't know. None of us who were there at the time knew either. It was a mystery in the dressing-room and none of us could quite grasp that it had happened. Joe's reign had not lasted long – but he had protected the basic beliefs at the club. He had kept the Anfield machine ticking over and, as well as the trophies he won in that incredible first season, that was vital to the club. And vital to all of the players. The respect for Joe never wavered in that dressing-room.

Then, in stepped Kenny. And while Joe had had Bob Paisley's example in making the transition from coach to manager, Kenny had no one to follow. I've said how difficult it must have been to step from the boot room to the manager's office – to go from the pitch to that office required someone special. I doubt if anyone other than Kenny Dalglish could have done it. Certainly he handled it better than anyone else would have been able to.

The man is a complete one-off. He moved into the job and managed to maintain the proper balance about things. After all, he was still there as a player – which made it doubly difficult – and he was being asked to take over in the wake of the Heysel disaster and after a season when the club had not won a trophy. And that had not happened to the club for nine long, success-laden years.

I reckon Kenny has done so well in the job because he is such a single-minded person. I could never have done what he has done. If Liverpool had asked me I would have told them, "No way". I know I could not have done the two jobs – probably I couldn't have done the one job as manager after having been a player there one day and then the boss the next. I couldn't have handled it. Kenny did. And he did so superbly. There he was, one of the lads one day and then in charge of them 24 hours later. Yet he steered a path for himself down a very difficult middle road. I had no idea that Kenny was to be manager. No one, apart from Kenny himself and the board, did. It came out of the blue. I didn't expect it because I still saw Kenny as an important player for the team. The thought of a player manager hadn't struck me, and for a club as big as Liverpool it was, I suppose, a bit of a gamble. Or it would have been if the candidate had been someone else. Dalglish was the one man who could take on the double role. He was, when I sat down to think about it, the outstanding candidate for the job.

Maybe others thought differently but the basic feeling among the lads was that Kenny was the right man. OK, Phil Neal fancied himself for the job. I think that he thought he was going to get it. Maybe he believed that he had been promised some kind of job with the club, and when Kenny got the manager's job his nose was out of joint. He would never have been, in my line of thinking, fit to be the manager. I could never have seen him handle things the way Kenny has done. He was the single voice in protest in the dressing-room when Kenny took over and the way that little incident was handled showed exactly how Kenny was going to handle the whole job.

The first day Kenny met the players as manager he simply told us that the situation had changed and that from now on we should call him "Boss". Only one player refused to accept that – Phil Neal. That was predictable, I suppose, but Kenny took it all on board without any great fuss. He pulled him aside, told him that this was to be the way things were, and that was that. It was sorted out quickly and without any great fuss. That's Kenny's way. He had to show everyone that he was now in charge but he was able to do it with the right attitude. He had an air about him where he did not go too overboard the one way. He didn't throw his weight around too much, nor was he too lenient with the lads. That had been the hardest thing and I know that Phil Neal would not have been able to do it with the same ease that Kenny did.

It has been difficult in many ways for me. Kenny is a friend of mine. We live close to each other in Southport and we have been close since he came down from Celtic to join the club. Our families are close, too – but I recognised early on that this was not going to influence him in any way. I suppose people, including some of the other players, watch closely to see if I'm favoured in any way. But I'm not. There are some things he has said to me in team talks and in post-mortems that have hurt – and often I've not been too happy about these remarks. But that is a manager's job. He has to do that and I have always accepted it. Not once have I tried to take any liberties, or to impose on our friendship in any way. I wouldn't do it and Kenny wouldn't wear it if I did. I have never met anyone who is as single-minded as he is about football. And about all aspects of his life. He knows exactly what he wants and he knows what he has to do to get that.

He made me captain, of course, and perhaps there were people who saw that as an old pals act. It wasn't. It could never have been because Kenny isn't made that way. It just would not be something that he would do. It would have been out of character. I don't know why he did pick me to be the club captain and I've never once asked him. But, knowing him, I would anticipate that if I did ask I would be told that he thought I was the right man for the job at that time. There would not be any fancy reasons, or any fancy talk. He would simply tell me straight out because he doesn't know any other way. I think life would have been considerably more difficult for me if I had believed for a second that I was being picked because we were mates. It would have made it harder for me to do the job as captain – and, of course, it would have made it harder for Kenny to do the job as manager. The authority he showed from the very beginning when he sorted out Phil Neal would have been undermined. He would never have risked that for an off-field friendship.

For instance, he was friendly with Alan Kennedy, who also happened to be my room-mate. But soon after Kenny took over Alan was on his way out of the club, back to his native north-east and a transfer to Sunderland. The fact that he was a mate didn't count. Kenny had decided that it was the right time for

Alan to move on from the club, and that was it. Phil Neal went at around the same time and that had always been on the cards since the dressing-room incident. But if Kenny had felt it was right for the club to keep him, then that would have been the case. I'm convinced of that. Personal reasons don't come into the decision-making process. He is very like Bob Paisley in that the good of the club comes before anything.

There is more than a little of Bob's ruthless touch in Kenny. He is not in the business of being pally with the players – a manager cannot afford that luxury. Bob Paisley and Joe Fagan, of course, didn't have that kind of problem because their respective ages distanced them from the players. I think that's why Kenny has taken the same ruthless road that Bob and other top managers have followed. It's the only way if you are to be good at your job. That really ruthless streak in his outlook makes it certain that he will be as successful as any manager who has had the job before him.

When it comes to my turn to be axed then I know that he will not think twice about it. In truth, the fact that we have been friends for around ten years might make him even harder on me. He might want to avoid the finger pointing that would suggest that he was unfairly favouring me. It's the only way for a manager to operate. If he shows any softness, any weakness, then he might lose out himself. As a manager he could suffer. And if the manager suffers then the team can suffer too. All Kenny is concerned about is success for Liverpool Football Club. He follows so steadily in Bob's footsteps as regards that.

I know that he has been criticised, and some of that has been totally unfair. There is a strong bond of loyalty which runs through the club, and when anyone gets stick from outside then we tend to band together. That happened when Kenny came under the cosh from the Press. We were all hurt. Some journalists, and others, too, were judging him wrongly. Just because Kenny doesn't stand on ceremony and can occasionally be lacking in diplomacy, doesn't mean that he is wrong. He just doesn't suffer fools gladly. And he won't hang around when he believes that someone is talking rubbish. In fact he is more likely to tell them what he thinks.

What the snipers wouldn't know about Kenny, of course, is that they won't change him if he believes he is right. He can be stubborn that way. If he is convinced that a certain course of action is the right one, then he will stick to his guns.

For instance, he was criticised for playing the 'sweeper' system – but we had done that under both Bob and Joe. Yet Kenny was accused of changing the Liverpool style. OK, it has been a little bit wayward when we have used that set-up at Anfield, but away from home it has been a success for us on a lot of occasions. Some people just don't know what they want. We went to Watford one day, used the 'sweeper' tactic and won 3-1 at Vicarage Road, and yet there were still those who said that we were not the old Liverpool, that we would never be a success playing this way and that the system was so defensive that we would never score goals the way we had before. Yet we did score three goals away from home in the First Division, and that isn't something you can do every other week. When we first used the system under Kenny's managership none of us had problems with it. After all, we could all fit into the set-up. Gary Gillespie could sweep on the right, I could sweep on the left, and Mark Lawrenson was there to handle things in the middle. It was a set-up that we enjoyed as defenders and it can still be used at times when we go away from home.

Kenny does things his way. If he wants to alter things a little then he does it, and with a double in his first year under his belt and another title since, then how can anyone argue with him? He does the job a little differently from Bob and Joe, but then that's natural. For a start he is younger than they were – and he remained a player for the early part of his managerial career. Also, he didn't graduate from the boot room so maybe that legendary little room along the corridor at Anfield doesn't mean quite so much as it once did. As players, none of us went in there. Maybe we would pop our head round the door to see if there was a sandwich lying handy after a game. But we would never sit down to talk to Ronnie Moran and the others. That just wasn't done. So Kenny works things a little differently – but the basic approach to things stays the same. That is

New man in the dug out. Kenny Dalglish soon after taking over as Liverpool manager.

unchanging. One of the old sayings around Anfield is "First is first – second is nowhere". We have no time for being runners-up in any competition. That's failure. It was failure under Bob. Failure under Joe. And it remains failure under Kenny. That will never alter.

I would imagine, too, that it's a saying that has reached Ibrox Stadium and the Rangers players in the last couple of years since Graeme Souness took over as team boss there. Perhaps Graeme has picked up other things from the seasons he spent with Sampdoria in the Italian First Division, but I doubt if any of them would replace the teachings of Anfield. Yet I was surprised when I heard the news that Graeme had been appointed player manager of Rangers. I knew that, like Kenny, if anyone could do the double job then it would be Graeme. And I also recognised that if anyone could make Rangers one of the biggest clubs in Europe, then, again, it would be Graeme. But I just didn't think Graeme would go into the demanding job of club manager. I thought that he would play for another year in Italy and then, maybe, go into the Swiss First Division. The standards are still reasonably high there, the rewards are good and the demands are less. It would have been an ideal way for Graeme to ease himself away from the pressures and out of the game. But then I also remembered that he used to say to me that as you get older every game you play is a bonus. I can remember telling him I was ready to give it all up after a bad game, or maybe after a few bad games. Graeme would simply point out that once you had to stop playing, then the game would be hard to replace. I realise now what he was talking about. After nearly 600 first-team games for Liverpool I reckon every one I play now is that bonus Graeme talked about.

Possibly, like so many other players, Graeme could not stand the thought of a week without football filling his time. I see now that he is finding it just as hard as Kenny has done to hang up his boots. He talked of only playing in emergencies – but without anything really serious happening he has been making regular appearances. I know that he will be fit and I know, as well, that his talents won't have withered. Nor will his

determination. He used to amaze me. When things got really
hard out there on the field then you knew that Graeme would be
there in the thick of it. He would be ready to help out anyone in
the team – he and Kenny used to be able to will the rest of us on
to win. Like Kenny, he has that single-minded quality and I'm
certain that the Rangers players will find him equally ruthless
in his dealings with them. After all, he came up in the same
hard school.

*Phil Thompson and Phil Neal share a joke at a club party. But Neal wasn't
laughing when Kenny Dalglish was made boss.*

I was impressed by the way he approached the job initially.
Down he came to England to buy two of the top defenders in
the First Division – something that was never heard of before.
Players like myself and Kenny would come south, but who
went north? No one! Then, suddenly, Terry Butcher,
England's regular centre-half, had gone to Ibrox and so had
Chris Woods, the number two international goalkeeper. Now
Gary Stevens is there too and Bobby Robson has to make trips
north to Glasgow to check on three of his key defensive stars.
It's something I would never have imagined possible. And I
doubt if anyone but Graeme would have had the personality

and the confidence to make the transfer moves and then to follow them through to such an extent that the whole Scottish scene has been revolutionised. You cannot help but admire the style with which he has approached the job.

I know that Rangers fans always believed that their club was one of the best in the world. Graeme is clearly intending to make these boasts come true. The only thing that has surprised me is that Graeme found himself in trouble when he went back home. It amazed all of us when the news came down that he had been ordered off in the first game he played in the Premier League. Then it happened twice more and I doubt if any player at Anfield could believe it. Graeme never got himself in any serious trouble when he was with Liverpool. He was not ordered off. He was rarely booked and it just seemed incredible that he could suddenly find himself a marked man back home in Scotland.

Graeme Souness – with champagne – but "just another Jock" according to Souness.

Maybe "marked man" is the right expression. I can only assume that Graeme was the target for opposing players and maybe for some referees as well. Even then it is hard for all of us who played alongside him so often to accept that he can find himself in so much hot water. I can remember hard games in the First Division when Graeme refused to fall for players who were trying to land him in bother. I can remember difficult games abroad when Graeme was the target for a lot of abuse but walked away from trouble. I would always have said that he was far too clever to allow himself to be "conned" into the kind of action which gets players sent off. If you can negotiate almost ten years at the top of the First Division and the same time in Europe, and add two years in the intensely competitive and often physical Italian First Division, without trouble, then questions have to be asked about trouble only suddenly arriving in his career. Perhaps the referees in Scotland are stricter than anywhere else in Europe. Perhaps the arrogance which Graeme has always carried on field with him antagonised both players and officials. I don't know the answer – but I do know Graeme. And for him to be ordered off three times was a major shock to me. And to everyone else at Liverpool. We just didn't believe it possible.

CHAPTER SEVEN

World Cup Disaster and Disappointment

IF I HAVE any really big regrets in my career then these surround Scotland and the international games I have missed. Some, admittedly, because of injury, others because I was not chosen to play. Playing alongside Kenny Dalglish and Graeme Souness for so long and watching them win honour after honour, my own disappointments became more and more acute. My international career spanned nine years – and as far as I'm concerned it is now drawing towards its close – and I won just 26 caps. Obviously that hurt at times – and at no time more than the last big disappointment I suffered. That was when Alex Ferguson, now Manchester United manager but then bossing Aberdeen and also the Scotland World Cup team, dropped me from the squad which was heading for Mexico.

Possibly that was the biggest blow in my entire career. I was convinced that I would be going to Mexico and everyone else was convinced that I would be making the journey to the 1986 World Cup finals – the fourth finals in succession that Scotland had taken part in. Kenny Dalglish, who was also set to be going to Mexico before injury hit him, was also telling me that I was a certainty to be included. Personally, I knew that I was playing well, probably better than at any previous time for Liverpool. But my form at Liverpool didn't always seem to impress the different Scottish team managers.

I hadn't been playing in the international side but I had been included in the various squads around that period. I could understand Alex Ferguson sticking to his club partnership of Alex McLeish and Willie Miller for a fair amount of the time because it's only natural that players are happy playing alongside their club-mates. But, even allowing for that, I did think that this time I would be going to Mexico, and I'm not a player who is given to believing that I'll be picked for this team or that team. I'm inclined to be a little pessimistic about things at times . . . maybe it would have been easier to take if that downbeat side of me had surfaced around the time of the Mexico squad being named.

I had been in the original 40 players named by Alex Ferguson and we were all aware that he had to whittle that number down to the 22 men travelling. When I journeyed up to Hampden to play in a testimonial the Scottish Football Association had granted Kenny I thought I was in. Twelve hours later I began to suffer my first pangs of doubt. Going up on the plane on the Saturday from London with Steve Nicol and Kenny I was feeling great. We had just clinched the First Division title at Stamford Bridge – and this was one of the times when I had been fairly sure we were going to miss out on the flag. Don't ask me why, it was just one of these nagging hunches you sometimes get. Usually when we had won titles before I had seen them coming from six or seven games off. But, for some strange reason, this time had been different. I had worried over it until that day at Stamford Bridge, and then suddenly we had done it and I can't tell you the relief I felt.

Anyhow, we booked in at the Grosvenor Hotel and I had a few celebration drinks there with Stevie and my brother, John, and went to bed early. Celebrations were cut down because we had the game to play for Kenny at Hampden the following afternoon. I woke early and thought I would go out to get the Sunday papers and see what the reports on the Chelsea game were like. But the reports on that match were forgotten over breakfast as another article in one paper caught my eye. "Unlucky players who will miss World Cup", it went – and there I was named as one of the players who would be staying at home! They've made a mistake here, I thought. Then I looked at another paper and there it was again. I soon realised that all the newspapers seemed to have the same story – and I also knew that all of them would not be wrong.

The doubts were invading my mind now and Mexico was receding into the far distance as I left for Hampden and the match. There were two teams of Scotland players, one bossed by Alex Ferguson and the other by Tommy Docherty. I was in the Doc's team which was really Kenny's own select side. Now, one of the surest signs that you are in trouble in this game is when a manager stops speaking to you. Ask any player about that. When the boss starts to ignore you, then you know that you are going to be in for it. At Hampden I got the message. Alex Ferguson blanked me there. He didn't look at the road I was on and I realised that the stories in the Sunday newspapers had been leaked. I was going to be out and I had only a few days to prepare myself for the chop which was going to come.

Before all of this Alex Ferguson had said that the disappointed players would be told on Wednesday before the squad was officially announced. My phone rang that Wednesday, he was on the other end, and I knew what was coming. There was only one thing he could be phoning me for – and that was to deliver the bad news. I can remember him saying, "I have some bad news for you. I'm not going to be taking you to Mexico." That was it, the message I had been dreading from the previous weekend. But at least I had had some chance to prepare myself to accept what Alex Ferguson was telling me. I told him, "You have to make that decision and I know that you can take only 22 players. You can't take everyone."

I think he was surprised at my reaction, the way I had taken it so calmly. In fact, I still believe to this day that he had phoned David Speedie before calling me and had got a bit of a mouthful

Alex Ferguson who left Alan Hansen out of the Mexico World Cup finals.

from the wee man. He had not been the slightest bit philosophical or understanding about it. He was unhappy and he told the team manager just how unhappy he was. Anyhow, Alex then went on about how he had to be loyal to players and how hard it had been for him to make the decision, and I interrupted him then. "Look," I said, "if you're not picking me, you're not picking me. That's the way things go. All the players you are taking with you to Mexico are good players and there's nothing we can do about it now." Then he answered: "It's a terrible decision I have had to make and I feel rotten about this."

After that he asked me if I would be available if anyone was injured or took ill or whatever before the squad arrived in Mexico. I said I would and the conversation was over. Now I had to make my own phone calls. I had to tell my dad and my brother John – even though I was gutted by the whole thing. After that I phoned Kenny to tell him and he was the same – he could not take it in to start with. He came round to the house that night with a bottle of champagne but we had the FA Cup final against Everton at Wembley looming a few days later and I turned down that chance to drown my sorrows a little bit.

There were suggestions later that I was left out because I was injured, and I don't really know how all that came up. It was not true. At least, I did have an injury, but it would not have affected me in the slightest if I had gone to Mexico. I had been playing right through the season for Liverpool with the injury, which was a torn muscle at the foot of my knee. All I had to do was take anti-inflammation tablets before a game and the injury didn't worry me one little bit. I had played 62 games that season without having a problem and the surgeon told me emphatically that I could have played 262 games and it still would have made no difference! I could have kept on playing for as long as I wanted without having any surgery performed on the leg. There was never the possibility of any permanent damage being done. However, with Mexico now out of my reach I did go into hospital. I went in for the operation on the Thursday following the Cup final. I came out of hospital on the

Friday with the minor surgery having been a success – and having been told that the only problem which could exist was if I did too much before the stitches had time to heal. On the Sunday I was playing golf. So you can see that the injury I was suffering from would not have worried me the least little bit if I had been selected for the Mexico squad!

But I don't hold any grudges because I missed the games there. I just feel the deep hurt that any player knows when he has missed important matches. I had felt that before with Liverpool, but this time I think I suffered more than ever before. In a club sense you miss a big game through injury and within a few days you can be looking forward to the next match and the next challenge. The World Cup only arrives every four years and I was fully aware that Mexico was my last chance of making another appearance at soccer's greatest showpiece. So it hit me hard when the games actually kicked off in Mexico.

Earlier I had been able to shrug it off a little bit. I can remember going in to Anfield and breaking the news to the lads, and saying to Stevie Nicol that I wouldn't be with him. He didn't believe me. The rest of the lads didn't believe me either. They thought it was some kind of a wind-up. Then, after training, at around midday, the Liverpool Press corps arrived at the ground and began to ask me how it felt being left out. That brought it home to them that I had not been kidding around. But telling them was easy compared to the agony I felt sitting at home when the finals started and the games were on television and I had nothing else to think about. Before that I could push the disappointment to the back of my mind because I had the Cup final to concern me and then I had the double win to console me. The Scotland decision seemed a little simpler to accept. Then when the kick-off for the games came around it swept over me again when I realised that the rest of the Scottish lads were over there taking part in the World Cup and I was left sitting at home in Southport watching it all on the box. That's when the real disappointment hit, that's when I knew that my solitary visit to the finals in Spain in 1982 was to be the only time I'd played in the finals of the World Cup tournament. I hadn't been in the frame at all in 1978 when Scotland went to Argentina. In Spain I played all three times in the opening group games, against Brazil and against Russia. Now, in 1986, when I captained Liverpool to the League and Cup double, I was left at home kicking my heels. That also meant that the abiding memory for most Scotland fans of my World Cup performances would be the disaster in Malaga against the Russians when Willie Miller and myself collided as millions of people watched the game on television and the Tartan Army watched in horror from the terracings of the Malaga stadium. Their horror was matched by my own – and probably by Willie's as well. It was one of those unbelievable happenings, a crazy incident which may have cost us qualification to the next stages of that World Cup. Yet, even after our spectacular "crash", the team manager Jock Stein came out and said that two of his best players had collided, and by saying that he was making it clear publicly, as he did to us personally, that he was not ready to write us off as a partnership.

I have never watched the tapes of that game. I don't have to. The details of the embarrassing collision which was such a disaster for Scotland, for me and for Willie are etched all too clearly in my mind. The basic problem, of course, was the old familiar one you tend to come up against when you are playing in an international team and forming a partnership with another player who operates in a different setting from you at club level. It isn't always easy to adapt, particularly when you are both used to playing in a specific way game after game, week after week throughout a domestic season. I would be playing one way for 70-odd games and then would have to try to make little alterations here and there for a handful of internationals. You can do it – and Willie and I did do it and have done it since then – but unless you have absolutely superhuman concentration then there are always moments when you slip back into your club style and that does the international team no good at all. That's what happened in Spain and this was the scenario: I was used to the Liverpool way where a defender stood his ground and if a forward was going to run past then you allowed that to happen before the ball was played through because you knew he would be offside. That's how we did things at Anfield and it worked for us. With Scotland I could not do that because Willie was used to a defensive set-up where he tucked in behind and played as the last man in defence. Basically the problem was that we came from such differing styles so that if I did let someone run on, instead of finding him offside I would see Willie standing around ten yards behind me. It caused us obvious worries because at the times when we were both playing our normal club roles it just wasn't working for us. Possibly I should have changed completely and sat back there alongside Willie, but it isn't as easy as it sounds to break the habits of a near-lifetime.

Dramatic action as Alan Hansen is thwarted by two opponents in this attacking move.

Anyhow, this particular time I am picking up their winger, Shengalia, out on their left-hand side – almost out on the touchline, in fact. The ball has been played over my head and I've turned to chase it back towards my own goal. I know that the Russian is behind me and there is no way that he is going to get the ball ahead of me. Then I see Willie running out towards us and I'm hoping that he gets between me and the goalkeeper and all I have to to do is pass the ball to him. But before we know what has happened, the two of us are still running for the ball and we have collided and the ball has gone loose and Shengalia is breaking through on goal with only Alan Rough to beat.

It was one of the worst moments I've known on a football field as I saw him going through to score and there we were 2-1 down towards the end of the game. Graeme Souness did get a tremendous equaliser – but that was not enough, and instead of going on into the next group of games we were heading home while the Russians travelled to Barcelona.

In all honesty I don't think it would have happened if I had been playing as 'sweeper'. And you can take that any way you want to. Afterwards I kept reading in the newspapers that it was not Willie's fault – so therefore I was catching the blame for the whole Keystone Kops incident. Everyone is entitled to their opinion but there is no way that I feel inclined to take the blame for the mix-up. I have my own view of the muddle and if I had been sweeper then I would have played things, I hope, a little differently from Willie. It's just a basic difference in approach. I would have tried to step in and clear the danger in another way.

No matter who was to blame it was a tragedy for the team. There we were out again, failing to qualify on goal difference for the third time in succession when we could have gone on. All I wanted to do was get off that pitch as soon as possible, get away from the scene of the crime, if you like. My room-mate in Spain was Davie Provan, and he tried to console me with a few beers that night, but even now, though it's such a long time ago, it's hard to push the incident to the back of my mind. Whenever I talk about it I can still see Willie coming towards me, and then I can remember, too, the realisation hitting me that a collision was unavoidable.

I played a few times with Willie after that in the Scotland

team and I don't think that particular goal loss and the daft way it happened scarred my career too much. I certainly had no qualms about lining up with Willie again and I don't think he had any about playing alongside me. Certainly a club partnership is always going to be better, but there was no earthly reason why Willie and I shouldn't have been able to play together. But then the talking started and there were suggestions that the two of us just couldn't get things going between us. That made it all the harder for both of us, I'm sure. Strangely, though, Willie and I have never talked about that clash. It's as if the memory still hurts too much.

We even managed to end up on the winning side together in the very next game the team played after the World Cup matches in Spain. It was a friendly at Hampden against East Germany and we won 2-0. I think the goals were from John Wark and Paul Sturrock, and I'm certain that Willie and I teamed up OK. At least the East Germans didn't score!

Following that game we kicked off a European Championship bid – and that's when some of the troubles hit me again. We went to Switzerland and lost 2-0 and the good things which had happened against the East Germans didn't occur too often that night in Berne. I was still in for the next game against Belgium in Brussels – and we were so unlucky to lose that match 3-2, especially as Kenny Dalglish scored one of the finest goals of his career and Frank Gray missed a penalty. The partnership at the centre of the defence changed a little in that one – I was with Alex McLeish. Then in the next match I was back with Willie. We failed to beat the Swiss and I was subbed when Alex McLeish came on to set up the club pairing once more.

After that I kind of disappeared from the scene. Injuries were involved; European Cup finals kept us out of some games; and Jock Stein seemed content to use a club partnership which was successful for him. To some extent, too, dropping out of sight after that game against the Swiss when we could only draw at Hampden was my own fault. At that time I knew I wasn't playing all that cleverly at club level, and so my confidence was at rock bottom. I was struggling through week after week but I didn't feel that I was playing the way I should be. Basically I was just going through a really bad period. I was on a downer and my trouble is that when I'm like that, when my confidence has slipped away down low, then I find it hard to lift myself. I find it hard to get going, hard to shake off the feeling that you are going out there to have a stinker!

That's been one of the biggest blights on my career. When I'm low on confidence I cannot always haul myself back to form the way other players can do it and, worst of all, I can look as if I'm not trying. Not always, but just at times, people think I'm not interested, not trying, and that I should be able to do something about it. That was one of these times towards the end of season 1982-83.

Maybe I was a little bit unlucky that Jock Stein did keep on picking me then, maybe it was his way of showing faith in myself and Willie after the Malaga mix-up. I don't know – but I do know he did continue to select me even though I was having a personal nightmare at club level. The more I tried, the worse I seemed to become, and whenever a ball was played past me on the field I just couldn't cope. I just wasn't able to handle it. The second Swiss game arrived at one of the worst times for me as regards my confidence. I knew that I hadn't done myself any favours but I wasn't prepared for the stick the fans started to give me. I mean, they started it all at the warm-up. It was pretty unpleasant. There you are up to play for your country and you are getting abuse from your own fans. And the way my confidence was that was all I needed. I was nervous enough getting ready for that game in the dressing-room. By the time I went through this ordeal at the warm-up I was really apprehensive. It did nothing to ease my nerves, I can tell you that!

It was a long time after that before I was back in the team, though I was included in the various squads of players for the different internationals by both Jock Stein and Alex Ferguson. But I missed a close season tour to Canada, which was more or less designed to get team understanding built up, and Alex and

Aberdeen star Willie Miller whose collision with Hansen brought World Cup disaster in Malaga against Russia.

Willie played together then. At club level they were successful and it was easy to understand Big Jock not wanting to disturb things too much in a vital part of the team.

There was one occasion when he announced that I was the "best centre-back in Britain" – but I still could not force my way back into the team. That became a frustrating time for me. I would be selected for the squad, travel to Glasgow or go abroad, and then not be played. But it's something you learn you have to accept – and at times expect – in an international set-up. It's not always easy to get into a World Cup team – even when you are skippering your club to the League and Cup double in England!

Again, though, I found it hard to blame anyone. I muffed my own chances and by the time my form returned I was battling against a club pairing which he was probably right not to break up.

If Gary Gillespie and I had been playing together in the same way as Willie and Alex were, then perhaps we would have been handed the same chance. But that has come too late to resurrect my career, particularly when you add the problem I have had with injuries.

The new team boss, Andy Roxburgh, who was appointed after Mexico, selected me initially for the three opening European Championship games, and then after the Hampden loss to the Republic of Ireland I dropped out of the picture once more and my knee began to play up. Deep down I worried in case my international career was over. If I had not been injured in the last pre-season during a tour game in Spain, then perhaps I would have had another chance to help Scotland in the current World Cup qualifying games. The Press were making suggestions about that and my knee had responded to a close season of rest – and then came the damage to the other knee. I was sitting at home nursing an injury when Scotland went to Norway and won.

If I had been given another chance then it would have meant a career being resurrected – but I would also have expected that to happen on a more or less temporary basis. I don't honestly expect to add many more caps to the 26 that I have won. Deep down, when I consider my international career realistically, I admit that it should have turned out a lot better – and I have to take some of the responsibility for that. It certainly wasn't always as disastrous as Malaga and the game against Russia, but it could have been and should have been better – and longer. I would have thought that, taking everything into consideration, I should have been able to win somewhere around 60 or 70 caps. I didn't and there is no use spending time now crying about it. All I'll say is that it would have been nice if things had been a little different; nice if I had been able to look back on more than just that single World Cup finals in Spain in 1982; nice if I had been able to hoist my number of caps to at least over 50 and have pushed myself into the Hall of Fame that the Scottish Football Association have. But, for all kinds of reasons, that wasn't meant for me, and it will remain a major regret when I look back at my career.

Hansen, after a game, and another victory.

CHAPER EIGHT

The Glory Days in Europe

THE LOSS OF European football following the Heysel disaster, which I will talk about at length elsewhere in the book, has been a devastating blow to those of us who had played for so long in the various Continental competitions. Until the tragedy in Brussels I had played in eight consecutive European Cup competitions, while other players had maybe picked up experience in the other tournaments with other clubs. I'm sure I am speaking for all the players when I say how badly I've missed being in Europe. For myself, I had always looked on the European Cup as something that little bit special, possibly because it had always seemed away beyond me when I was starting out as a player with Partick Thistle. With all due respect to the European Cup Winners Cup and the UEFA Cup, the big one was always the Champions Cup. That looms above the others. It is the blue riband of European football. You know that if you can win that trophy then you are the best team in Europe because, after all, it is the Cup for champions.

It is also the tournament which has thrown up its own legends down through the years. I grew up in Sauchie at a time when Real Madrid and Benfica were the teams whose names were synonymous with the trophy. The players who were always mentioned were Puskas and di Stefano and Gento and Eusebio and Coluna and Germano. Then came the Italian clubs, AC Milan and Inter Milan with Suarez and Facchetti, with Rivera and Maldini. And, of course, in Scotland there were the Lisbon Lions, that famous Celtic team guided to their triumph by Jock Stein when no one gave them a chance of winning the Cup in 1967.

As a youngster I looked at all those famous names, and all those famous clubs, and the European Cup seemed light years away from me. Yet within a year of going south I was playing in the final of that tournament for the first time – and winning a medal at Wembley! All my mates were back in Sauchie, gathered round the telly with a few cans of beer, and I was out there on Wembley playing against the Belgian champions, Bruges. I was only twelve months away from the village. It was unbelievable and yet, approaching the game, it seemed to me as if it was going to be an anticlimax. Don't ask me how that was – probably it was because we had been made favourites to win. Odds-on favourites. Possibly, too, it was because the game was being played in England, at Wembley, instead of in strange surroundings abroad. These feelings, though, didn't persist for too long.

My bottle collapsed about 45 minutes before the game. That's when it hit me for the first time, and by the time I was walking out of the tunnel on to the field I was a nervous wreck – a condition I remained in until I went back across the field with Terry Mac at the end of the game to collect my medal.

It wasn't surprising really that it should eventually hit me that way. That was my first season in the first team and I played only 19 games as Bob Paisley began to reshape the side which had won the European Cup for the first time the year before. Then, in Rome, with Kevin Keegan running the show, they had beaten the West German champions, Borussia Moenchen-gladbach, 3-1 with the goals coming from Terry McDermott, Tommy Smith and a Phil Neal penalty.

Neither Keegan nor Tommy Smith was to be in the

Wembley final and, in all, four players were *out* of the team which had given Bob that first-ever European Cup victory. Joining the two I have mentioned were Joey Jones and Ian Callaghan. But, of course, Kenny Dalglish had joined the club in the summer after Keegan's departure for Hamburg. And then Graeme Souness came in on a £350,000 transfer from Middlesbrough and Bob Paisley had put together a team which was to bring Liverpool more European Cup honours than even he could have imagined.

I played in the two second-round games – as holders of the trophy we had a first-round bye – against the East German champions, Dynamo Dresden, games which are always talked about by the backroom staff. In the first game at Anfield we stuffed them 5-1 and I managed to get myself on the score sheet along with Jimmy Case, who helped himself to a couple, Phil Neal with a penalty and Ray Kennedy. They never worried us, even though they did get one goal, and we went over there looking to have an easy time of it. We didn't. We were hit by a performance which the Anfield boot room still describe as one of the best they have ever seen in Europe. There was a stage where they wondered if the East Germans had been on some kind of stimulants. Certainly they were hyped up when they came out to face us that day. They seemed, honestly, to believe that they could win. The fact that they were four goals down from the first leg and the equally obvious fact that they had been outclassed in that game at Anfield had no effect on them whatsoever. They gave us a going-over and we were lucky to get away with a 2-1 defeat, with Steve Heighway scoring for us to relieve the pressure a little. It remains, to this day, one of the most talked-about European games by the old hands at Anfield. They frightened us – and not too many teams were able to do that when we were in command of a tie. It may not have been one of the most important games played at Liverpool down through the years, and yet because of the way they played it has gone down in the folklore of the boot room. I reckon it's mentioned more than some of the finals we played in.

I dropped back out of things for a bit after that. The next

A jubilant Terry McDermott. Hansen believes he should have won more caps for England than he did.

European game we played was the quarter-final, which was against Benfica and was several months after that trip behind the Iron Curtain. Graeme had joined the club by this time but had not been registered in time to play in the quarter-final stages. I made an appearance as substitute in the first leg in the Stadium of Light in Lisbon, where 70,000 fans saw us beat the Portuguese champions 2-1 with goals from Jimmy Case and Emlyn Hughes. I went on for Phil Thompson but Kenny was the only "Jock" on for the whole 90 minutes, and it was the same at Anfield when he scored his first European goal for the club in a 4-1 win. Joining him were Ian Callaghan, Terry Mac and Phil Neal. I remained a spectator and when the semi-finals came along and we were drawn against the West Germans from Borussia Moenchengladbach I had to be content with another view from the bench. Mind you, in the first leg of this repeat of the previous year's final Graeme had to sit it out with me until he was pushed on in the Neckar Stadium in Düsseldorf for Steve Heighway. The lads lost that first leg 2-1 but a Dave Johnston goal gave us all hope that we would go through to the final again. And knowing it was to take place at Wembley meant the lads had a real incentive when they went into the second leg of that semi-final against the West Germans at Anfield. Kenny scored again, so did Ray Kennedy and so did Jimmy Case.

We were on our way to Wembley. And that's when I was brought back into the picture. Kenny scored and he and Graeme and I shared our first taste of glory with the club and the first of the "Jock pictures" was taken. Bruges had a strong team, but a dour team. They were defensive and their coach Ernst Happel, the Austrian who managed so many clubs and countries in Europe, was determined that they would not be beaten easily at Wembley. They reckoned everything was stacked against them, that it was as good as a home game for us, and I suppose they were right. But it didn't make for a classic final. The goal from Kenny is my abiding memory of a match I think I played in a trance.

Bruges fielded a team packed with internationals from across Europe – they came from Belgium, from Holland, from

Denmark and from Austria. On the way to the final they had beaten such teams as Atletico Madrid and Juventus. And yet I think deep down we all knew that we were going to be able to win that night. It was the second half before a pass from Graeme eventually opened up the way for Kenny to score, and from then until the end we were able to play comfortably and achieve what we had set out to achieve – we had become the first British club to win the European Cup twice. It was something which had never been done before, and the next morning when I woke up in the Holiday Inn at Swiss Cottage – always our London HQ – I couldn't come to grips with the fact that I was one of the few Scots who owned a European Cup medal. I'd been told often enough about the one Bertie Auld had won, now I had one too and it was a good, warm, comfortable, if slightly unreal, feeling. It was another world, a whole, brave new world which I had been catapulted into. Now all I had to do was learn to enjoy it as it happened instead of moving around like a zombie with Terry Mac guiding me towards the Royal Box where the medals were handed out!

There was a gap then, a little bit of a three-year hiccup in our European glory – unfortunately interrupted by Brian Clough and his Nottingham Forest team, who had given notice that they were after us that same season. They beat us for the title as we were winning against Bruges, and beat us in the final of the League Cup too. It was their time, and they went on to equal us in Europe with two successive wins before we could hit back. To rub salt into the wounds they knocked us out of the European Cup in the first round when we were holders. That was a sore, sore blow to our pride and to our professionalism. We went two goals down to them at the City Ground and we never looked like scoring even once at our place. It was a tribute to them and to the way they played that they were able to frustrate us so successfully. There were other times when I felt we were unlucky, once in a League Cup game when Peter Shilton gave the finest goalkeeping display of his life – if not the finest goalkeeping display I've ever seen from anyone anywhere. There were other times when we would batter and batter away at them and come away wondering just what we had to do to win against them.

For a year or two it was as if they had an Indian sign on us. Cloughie has always been a little bit of a one-off and these were his finest days. Two European Cup wins plus all the successes he had at home and the ability to turn us over in so many vital games. He had good players, too. Little John Robertson was very underestimated. Robbo was a fantastic player but he was never given as much credit as he deserved. He was a tremendous outlet for them. They could be under pressure, switch the ball out to the left and Robbo would pick it up.

Forest then took up where we had left off in the European Cup. They went on to win the competition after beating us that year with a Trevor Francis goal in the final being enough to defeat the Swedish side Malmö in Munich. And the following year we were dumped in the first round again, this time from the Russians of Dinamo Tbilisi. Once more Forest carried the banner of the English First Division. They repeated their victory and equalled our record of two successive wins in the competition. This time they were able to beat Hamburg – whose team included Kevin Keegan – with a goal from John Robertson in Madrid.

By now, sensing that there was a real and dangerous challenge to what we had been hoping would be European supremacy for Liverpool, there was a period of regrouping and of rebuilding. Not drastic changes . . . but the kind of gradual changes which Liverpool seem able to make as the years go by without in any way affecting the family atmosphere at the club. If changes were going to have to be made, then they would be. But they were never disruptive. It was never as if the side was going to be torn totally apart. That was not the Anfield way. They would tinker here and tinker there until they got the magnificent machine they had created firing on all cylinders once more.

So, by this time, two years after we had last won the trophy, we started off on another quest to win it with only a few changes from the side which had won against Bruges at Wembley.

Emlyn Hughes had gone, while David Fairclough and Steve Heighway, a substitute at Wembley against Bruges, were slipping out of the picture. Alan Kennedy had broken through to make the left-back position his own, and little Sammy Lee was another who was a regular. Meanwhile, it was Forest's turn to taste the bitterness of a first-round defeat when they crashed out to the Bulgarians of CSKA Sofia, a team who were to arrive at Anfield in the quarter-finals. They lost 1-0 in Sofia and then, surprisingly, lost by the same score at their own City Ground.

A familiar sight in Liverpool as the Anfield team return home with a trophy. This is after winning the European Cup in Paris in 1981.

We had been drawn against the champions of Finland, Oulon Palloseura, and expected to win the tie easily. But we were only able to draw 1-1 away from home. Terry McDermott saved our blushes that day. In the second leg we ran riot. The poor Finns did not know what had hit them. There were, as usual, only two weeks between the two games, but our

performance was light years away from the one we had given on
their ground. Bob Paisley played exactly the same team, clearly
saying to us, "You made a mess of the first match – now show
what you can really do." We accepted the challenge. Graeme
Souness and Terry McDermott both helped themselves to
hat-tricks, David Fairclough grabbed two goals and Sammy
Lee and Ray Kennedy scored the others.

It was a rout and it pushed us into the second round and a
clash against the Scottish champions, Aberdeen, who, under
manager Alex Ferguson, were emerging as a major team in
Britain and in Europe. They had beaten Austria Memphis
Vienna in their first-round game – and it was a powerful side
from the Austrian capital, with almost half of the international
team in its ranks. But, then, Aberdeen had good players too.
Their central defenders Alex McLeish and Willie Miller were
both in the Scotland World Cup squad when Graeme and
Kenny and I had played alongside them. So, too, was little
Gordon Strachan, while Jim Leighton was already understudy
to Alan Rough in the Scotland goal.

I suppose we were favourites to win the tie but none of us –
especially the Jocks – were anything other than certain that this
would prove a difficult game. In the event it didn't. Although
Aberdeen were to mature enough to win the Cup Winners Cup
two years later, they did not have the European experience
under their belts that we did. That was Alex Ferguson's verdict
after the two-legged tie which saw us win 1-0 at Pittodrie and
then hammer in four goals against them when they made the
journey south to Liverpool.

I can still remember the goal Terry Mac scored up there in
Aberdeen. It was a gorgeous chip which was enough to give us
that first leg win and to imprint itself indelibly on my mind. No
one else at Anfield would have been able to score that goal. It
had Terry Mac's trademarks written all over it. He was a player
who never did get enough credit for the job he did at Anfield.
He was an exceptional player in an exceptional team and yet he
used to be overlooked. I don't know why. His touch was
brilliant. His passing was special. His runs from the middle of

the field were exceptional and he was a regular goalscorer. Yet he never hit the headlines, never seemed to catch the eye the way other players did. But if you ask the lads about the contribution he used to make in game after game, they would tell you just how good a player he was. Also how important he was to the team effort. Without a shadow of doubt he should have won more caps for England than he did. People used to try to say Terry drank too much, and he did like a few pints, more than a few on a Saturday night when the match was over. But it didn't affect him in the slightest. He could run the legs off anyone in the country and he was a great trainer. Maybe he didn't always like training. But he went out and did it and no one could beat him when he set his mind to working hard. Yet Terry finished up winning one less cup than I did. He managed to amass a total of 25 appearances for England. But, for my money, in that period at the end of the 'seventies and moving into the early 'eighties, he was the finest midfield man in the country. No one could touch him – and in Europe he was always one of our key players. His value to the side should never be underestimated. Terry Mac was one of those players who was probably more appreciated by his fellow professionals than by anyone else. And, perhaps, that was the way he liked it. Anyhow, his goal at Pittodrie left us in command of the tie, and while Aberdeen came south making defiant predictions I reckon they knew they would be under the cosh. That's how it turned out. Kenny and I managed to score one goal each, which pleased us probably more than usual because we knew we were showing the anti-Anglo brigade back home what we could do. Poor Willie Miller gave away an own goal and Phil Neal scored our other one. It turned out to be an easier tie than any of us had hoped for. I think that we caught Aberdeen just before they were hitting their peak – that possibly arrived when they went to Gothenburg to win the Cup Winners Cup. Unluckily for them they met us when we were at one of our peaks.

There was a determination about us that season, almost as if we were out to make sure that Forest were not going to be able to take over from us on the playing fields of Europe. We wanted that European Cup back at Anfield, back in the trophy room where it had sat for two years and back from the hands of our closest rivals in the First Division. So that was the mood we were all in when drawn against Aberdeen, and they suffered just as CSKA Sofia, conquerors of Forest, had done in the first leg. The Bulgarians, who had been able to win at the City ground as well as on their own patch, came to Liverpool confident of being able to do the same. Or of at least being able to hold us to a draw. It didn't work for them. That night Graeme Souness was inspired. He scored a marvellous hat-trick – his second in the competition that season – and we won 5-1 with our other goals arriving from that man MacDermott again and from Sammy Lee.

The poor Bulgarians were demoralised and they were not even able to lift their game when they met us in front of 65,000 of their own supporters in Sofia. David Johnston scored there and we were in the last four – and an illustrious group that was. Into the draw along with ourselves went Bayern Munich, Real Madrid and Inter Milan. All previous winners of the tournament, all teams studded with star names and top international players. It was at times like these, when you looked at that kind of opposition, that you could truly savour the full greatness of that competition.

When the draw was made that week we came out against the West German champions Bayern Munich, who had a whole crop of West Germany's top players including Paul Breitner and the fantastic Karl Heinz Rummenigge. We knew how difficult it would be to play against them. We knew just how well prepared they would be, how well organised they would be, and how patient they could be if either of the games called for that. But we didn't feel too concerned. It was a season when we had won the League Cup trophy for the first time – just a week before the first clash with the West Germans. That was a nice omen for us even though our title slipped away to be won by Aston Villa. Also, the whole thing about the European Cup was getting the chance to pit yourself against the best. It wasn't about winning by ten goals against a Finnish team. It was about how you handled yourselves when it came to the tournament élite. There was scarcely a more élite group than the champions of Italy, West Germany and Spain!

Somehow, though, the first leg of that semi-final at Anfield was a bit of an anticlimax. Our high-scoring run at home – we had managed 20 goals in our three previous ties at Anfield – came to a sudden and abrupt end. The West Germans arrived looking only for that draw – and they left happy. We realised that we had an awful lot to do in the return game at the Olympic Stadium in Munich. They had looked powerful at home in the competition too. In the second round, for instance, they had hammered five goals past Ajax of Amsterdam after having hit three against Olympiakos in the opening round and then grabbed two more against the Czech champions, Banik Ostrava, in the quarter-finals. On aggregate they had scored 19 goals in all in the competition – just a shade behind us. We had 22 goals, but half of that total had come against the hapless Finnish side in the opening matches.

A hat-trick. Bob Paisley plus cap along with the League Cup, Milk Cup and European Cup.

The only encouragement we did get from their record was that they had lost a goal at home to Ajax – but that was a poor crumb of comfort for us after we had failed to beat them at Anfield in front of a massive near-45,000 crowd. The odds were heavily against us, and before we headed for West Germany they became still worse when injuries wrecked the squad. The mightily experienced Phil Thompson was out. Alan Kennedy was out. Bob Paisley had to draft in Richard Money and Colin Irwin to take over from them in defence. If that wasn't enough, Kenny was injured after only seven minutes of the second-leg game and was forced to limp off. Another of the young players, Howard Gayle, came on to take his place.

Everything appeared to be against us. The odds were stacked high enough before the game so that when Kenny went off I'm convinced the West Germans were confident that this was to be their year of European glory. But somehow those youngsters all rose to the occasion magnificently. Bayern had trouble trying to deal with Howard Gayle and the two lads at the back were great. I was up against Rummenigge and I thought I played him well, even though he did get their goal. But when that came we were leading by a goal from Ray Kennedy. He had scored with just seven minutes left and it was in the final minute that the Germans were able to hit back. Too late, thank goodness. Rummenigge was one of the best players I ever came up against in Europe, though for me a whole host of big names didn't show up too well against us. My hardest times came in the First Division. Apart from the Bayern star, only perhaps Michel Platini really impressed me when I came up against him. He looked the part all the time.

That night in Munich was one of the great nights for the club. It was one of the few occasions when we were obvious underdogs, but all the European experience, all the tricks of the trade learned down through so many years of non-stop involvement were brought into use, and they carried us through even with all the problems we faced going into the game. Also, once the game had kicked off and Kenny was injured, lesser teams would have given up hope then and there.

That would have been it. A lot of players would have gone into hiding, would simply have chucked it. As I keep repeating, that's not the Liverpool way. We dug in, we battled and we won. It was on the away goals rule but it counted just as much as any other kind of result would have. We were back in the final and later we learned that it would be Real Madrid we would play in Paris the following month. They had beaten the Italians of Inter in the other semi-final and, again, we would find ourselves facing a side composed entirely of international players. But then, of course, the Spaniards must have been saying very much the same thing about us. At full strength we had our own share of international players – from England and Scotland!

When I look at some of the teams I have faced up to in Europe I sometimes wonder about the often repeated statement that when you step into the international team you go up a standard. You have to raise your game even higher than you would do in a club context. I don't know if that's right. It has been repeated so often that people simply accept it as the truth, but is it? Invariably I found myself playing against almost full international teams in Europe. It was the way it usually turned out. That Bayern side was packed with men who played for their country and it was the same when we came to face the men from Madrid in the final. As well as half-a-dozen men who played for the Spanish side, they also had the teak-tough West German sweeper Uli Stielike in the side they brought to Paris.

But this time we were better equipped than we had been in the semi-final in Munich. This time we did not have injuries to worry us on the run-up to the game, and we did not lose Kenny's vast influence in the opening minutes of the game. Our team that night was Clemence; Neal, Alan Kennedy; Thompson, Ray Kennedy, and yours truly; Dalglish, Lee, Johnston, McDermott and Souness.

I can remember coming out on to the field at the Parc des Princes and seeing a massive banner which the Spanish fans had draped over their end of the ground. I'd never seen anything like that in my life before. It seemed to cover the entire terracing, billowing in the breeze, and it added its own little bit to the atmosphere which we felt as we took the field that night. It was electric, because that Paris stadium is so compact that the whole atmosphere seems to build until it reaches a kind of crescendo. That's the way it was then and I'll never forget it. It seemed such a bigger occasion than the first European final had been at Wembley. Perhaps, too, that came because we were going into action against Real Madrid, the team who had dominated the competition during the early years of its existence. The great names of the past may have gone – though Ferenc Puskas was in the stadium to watch the game that night – but they had new faces, new sparkling talents to replace them and, they hoped, bring back the former glories. Their hopes were pinned on Camacho and Juanito and Santillana and del Bosque, and they believed that they were due to repeat those days of greatness the team had known when di Stefano and Gento and Puskas and the others thrilled the crowds in the Spanish capital.

If any club name dominates the European Cup then it is that of Real Madrid, because as well as winning the trophy more than anyone else they also had a reputation for winning it with style. They were the darlings, still, of all the neutrals, and we recognised that if we were to win then, apart from our own fans and others at home who would be watching the game on television, we would not be the most popular winners the tournament had known. We were playing against a legendary club – and unpopularity was the penalty we might have to pay. We were all willing to risk that. Naturally!

The best boost of all for us was that Kenny Dalglish was playing again. The knock he had taken against Bayern had been a particularly nasty one, and although there was a gap of six weeks between that match in Munich and our showdown with Real in Paris, there had been worries over him. He had not been able to play in any other games in between – but he was ready for this one. That lifted us, and must have had the Spaniards a little bit concerned. I'm sure they would have loved to be able

Hansen looks confident here as he strides forward to help his attack.

to take the field knowing that a person as vastly skilled and influential as Kenny was being left behind in our dressing-room. Eventually Kenny did have to go off in the second half, but it was typical of him that he would be able to go into such a game without match preparation and play as he did. Eight minutes from the end Alan Kennedy scored the single goal of the game. It was a spectacular shot and it gave us the European Cup for the third time, allowing us to join a select group of teams who had been able to secure that hat-trick. The others were Ajax and Bayern Munich – ironically enough it had been the West Germans we had defeated in the semis. And before that Bayern had knocked out the Dutch side.

It was not a classic final, but it was a great result for the club and it gave me my second European Cup medal. My wife Janet, who was pregnant, was not able to go to the final that year, and afterwards we had a party in my room to celebrate. Terry Mac was there, of course, and my dad and my Uncle John, as well as about 20 others. I always remember my dad and my uncle getting on to me because I was ordering champagne. They thought we should organise a "kitty" and everyone would chip in. So for a laugh I said, "OK, let's get a 'kitty' organised and we will get the bill up." They almost collapsed. It was for £830. They hadn't realised just how much champagne could cost in a Paris hotel. Terry and I were not caring too much what it cost by that time. We had won the European Cup once more and we were set for another crack at the tournament we all loved the following season.

That was to provide another setback when we lost to CSKA Sofia, our old rivals from Bulgaria, in the quarter-finals, and Aston Villa won it to strengthen the English hold on Europe's most coveted prize. Then the following year Hamburg won the trophy while we went out to the Polish team Widzew Lodz in a tie we all reckoned we might have won. Again it was a quarter-final exit, but the following season brought us one of our finest victories in the competition. And one of our most memorable campaigns when often we appeared to be written off. As always, we were able to come back . . ..

CHAPTER NINE

The Glory that was Rome

BY THE TIME this challenge came along, of course, Joe Fagan had taken over from Bob Paisley, but little changed in the preparations which the club made for their annual assault on Europe. Everything was worked out to the last detail. The backroom staff really did have European ties and everything which surrounded them, all the preparations, down to a fine art. It wasn't only how you played the games themselves. It was how you travelled and when you travelled and where you stayed and what you ate and how you trained for the game and how you approached the game. Every single thing was just right and I mean every single thing. Nothing was left to chance.

Some clubs talk about players having to acclimatise to conditions where they are playing . . . not Liverpool. We went out on the Tuesday afternoon to prepare for a game the following night. Maybe it was right for other people to go early, but it wasn't the done thing for Liverpool. The club wanted to keep us in our own surroundings for as long as possible. You were in the city where you had to play for one night only, if that was possible. Just in, to do the job, and out again.

We took our own food with us too and two chefs who were in

charge of preparing all the meals. We would even take oranges with us for half time and our own bottled water. There were absolutely no chances taken. I think all of us who were there remember half-time tea being thrown out by Bob Paisley in Lodz because he didn't want anyone to risk stomach upsets from water or anything which had been prepared over there. It might have seemed a little paranoid to outsiders but I think that perhaps in the early days in Europe Liverpool had learned that players can get stomach upsets, and that being away from home too long could make players perform below par. Whatever the reason, in all my time in Europe, we stuck by the same routines and I understand that Graeme Souness has followed the pattern with Rangers.

We had the same basic approach to the game when we went abroad too. We could take the field before the game and line up and wave to their fans, a long, slow arm wave. Terry Mac was the first one to do it, then I followed and eventually we were all doing it. It was just a little thing but it helped ease the tension which always builds up to an intense level before these games. After all, you are going out to play in front of a hostile crowd in some far-off corner of Europe, where sometimes 80,000 or so people can be watching. Anything to calm you down and give you a bit of a laugh helps. I know it helped me. So many people won't believe that I am affected by nerves because they reckon I look so calm. Not true. I may look calm on the outside but inside I'm very often a wreck. A complete and total wreck!

I reckon that I suffer more before games than most of the other lads do but I am maybe more successful at keeping it hidden. I used to think that the feelings which start to invade my mind as kick-off approaches would ease off the longer I had been in the game. But I've now found out that doesn't happen. I feel it before every game, that grip of tension which is so hard to get rid of. Naturally these European ties were always the worst because there would be so much at stake, so much riding on a single result. Or, and this would always cross my mind, so much damage could be caused by a single mistake. We would usually start some kind of wind-up in the dressing-room beforehand just to ease the atmosphere, have the lads laughing and so get a relaxed feel before going out and giving the orchestrated, so slow wave to the rival supporters. Thankfully, all these little ploys used to work. At least they did most of the time.

Then when the game started the tactic in the early stages was always the same. The plan was to take the sting out of the match. We would try to keep possession and myself and Graeme and Phil Thomson, for example, would try to pass the ball about at the back. That would keep it away from the opposition and allow us to feel our way into the game gradually. It also allowed our own confidence to build and, if it worked well, it would gradually quieten down their fans. Once you managed to dampen their enthusiasm the next thing you had to hope for was that they would begin to turn on their own players. When they got a little bit restless and started to jeer one or two of the opposition players then we knew we were onto a result. You see, when that happened, then players began to let their hearts take over from their heads. They would start to charge forward blindly and that eased the danger we might be facing. It wouldn't always work but it certainly saw us through a whole bundle of tough ties. Our instructions were mainly to hold the ball. If we didn't penetrate too much no one worried.

The backroom staff preached patience and so, when Joe took over that season from Bob and we were facing a trip to Bilbao in the second round after winning comfortably in Odense in Denmark in the first we knew the team talk would be the same as always . . . particularly when the Spanish held us to a 0-0 draw in the first leg of the game at Anfield. Clearly our scoring exploits against the Danes in the first round had been noted carefully in Bilbao, because while only a goal from Kenny Dalglish separated us in the first leg over in Odense it was a decisive win for us when the Danish champions came to Anfield. We scored five that night and the goals came from Kenny who scored two, Michael Robinson with two more and a Danish defender with an own goal. It had been a nice, comfortable opening for us and while we were doing our own business in our own way the Spaniards who were to meet us in round two had lost to Poznan in Poland by 2-0 before winning the return game 4-0 in their own stadium. They had been shaken by the loss of two goals away from home, they had seen our five goals against Odense and so they came to put up the shutters. Unfortunately for us they succeeded in doing so.

At any rate we went over to Bilbao and on their own ground we beat them 1-0 with a strike from Ian Rush. It was an important goal and an important victory. Most people had written us off but we always felt we had a chance because we had stopped them scoring at our place. Down through the years it has become increasingly important not to lose a goal at home. With the rule in the European tournaments that a goal scored away from home counts double in the event of a draw it is vital to stop the opposition scoring when they come to play at your ground. Then, you have to try to nick a goal when you go there. We did it this time, thanks to Rushy. And that catapulted us forward to the quarter-finals.

The second round of Europe always seemed a particularly important one for me. As well as the obvious matter of progressing in the tournament and a win in that round did put you into the last eight there was another advantage. The second-leg games would be over by early November and the next round was not played until March to avoid the winter shutdown which so many European nations have. So in the dark, cold, wet and windy days of December and January and February, you always knew that there was another round in Europe to look forward to. It was a great lift to realise that a glamour game and a chance of more European action and perhaps glory was still waiting for the team as you ploughed through the mud or skidded over the ice and snow.

Anyhow, disposing of Bilbao gave us a special lift that season because it turned out to be an enormously difficult tie. At Anfield they did not look a particularly brilliant team but they were disciplined and they held us. Quite frankly we knew that Bilbao is not the kind of place you would choose to go to look for a victory. If anyone was betting on that game they would have

European Cup final v. Roma.

had to fancy the Spanish side before us. It was a difficult journey and one fraught with dangers for us. So when Rushy scored and we went through our hopes of maybe taking the European Cup rose once again. The previous year's winners, Hamburg, had gone out to Dinamo Bucharest of Rumania. Roma had taken out our old rivals CSKA Sofia and the Scottish champions, Dundee United, had beaten the powerful Belgian side, Standard Liege. The ranks were thinning . . . although Roma, whose home ground would stage the final, had more to play for than most of us. A final in their own stadium! What could be better?

As always it was a formidable list of teams who made up the last eight. You invariably find that by this stage of the competition the easy touches have gone. The time to catch the "rabbits" is in the early rounds though even then there are occasions when you can be drawn against an unseeded side who have suddenly come good and have the potential to take the trophy. That had happened to us with Forest and with the Russian champions Dynamo Tbilisi, but it was hard to imagine picking up an easy draw when it came to the cream of the competition. The eight clubs that season boasted only two previous European Cup winners, ourselves and Benfica from Portugal. But the pedigree was still outstanding with Dundee United and Roma, Dinamo Bucharest and Dynamo Berlin, Dynamo Minsk and Rapid Vienna. For a start there were too many Eastern European teams for my liking. I don't think any player enjoys the thought of going behind the Iron Curtain for a tie and the last times we had been there had brought defeats from CSKA Sofia of Bulgaria and from the Polish team Widzew Lodz. Another journey to the east didn't look welcoming.

In the end when the draw was made we were paired with Benfica and that brought back memories of the time we had won the trophy at Wembley. We had played the Portuguese then – also in the quarter-finals – and we had won 6-2 on aggregate. It had been a famous victory for us and it was still one we savoured after all these years had passed. This time we could look on the draw as a kind of lucky omen for us, maybe a repeat win would also bring a repeat of that European Cup triumph in 1978. It's what we all hoped for.

At Anfield, however, the Portuguese team didn't play the game according to our script. Like Bilbao they came to defend but, unlike them, they didn't do it quite as successfully. Still, it was good enough to worry us and good enough to send them back home to Lisbon believing that they would get revenge for the previous quarter-final result. All we had to show after the first 90 minutes was a single goal – predictably enough it had come from Ian Rush. And predictably enough there was no shortage among those who were ready to write us off again. Just as they had done in the previous round when we could only draw with Bilbao. That was enough to get us going. We didn't need too much motivation for the return in the Stadium of Light. That night we gave one of our best-ever performances in Europe as far as I'm concerned. The semi-final in Munich against Bayern had been outstanding but it was mainly defensive because of our injury problems. This time we controlled the game from the start. Inside half an hour we were three goals up and even I could not believe that. It was an incredible performance the lads gave and I sat back in defence and enjoyed it. Every minute of it.

We went into the game looking on the Rushy goal as a cushion because we expected to be under the collar for most of the game. Instead that goal became a launching pad for a brilliant display from the team. Ronnie Whelan scored twice and the other goals game from Craig Johnston and Rushy, once more. The Portuguese international star Nene scored for them but they were demoralised. It was as effective and as magnificent a performance as I ever saw from the lads in Europe. It was one of those nights when things went well, when we had the seven or eight players on top form that you need for a great display. Few teams in Europe would have been able to live with us. It was also one of the best nights in Europe that I knew personally because I was able to relax and enjoy myself. There was very little real pressure on our defence and so we could sit back and enjoy what was happening in front of us. If only all of the games had been like that one!

Dundee United went through that night as well, defeating Rapid Vienna 1-0 with a goal from their striker Davie Dodds after having gone down 2-1 in the first leg in Austria. It was a good result and it proved that the little team from Tannadice had mastered the art of playing in Europe. They appeared to know the drill for playing abroad and we knew that they had good players as well as an impressive pedigree in other European competitions. As we waited for the draw for the semi-finals the speculation was growing that there might yet be an all-British final and that Roma might have to suffer the indignity of being spectators at that final. Certainly the way was left open for that to happen when we were drawn against the Rumanians of Dinamo Bucharest who had managed to defeat the Russians from Minsk in their quarter-final. It was United who had to go in against the men from Rome.

The Rumanians had been to Anfield before – 13 years earlier in the old Fairs Cup, the tournament which was renamed the UEFA Cup. Liverpool, then, had won 4-1 on aggregate before going into the semi-finals and a defeat from Leeds United. That result obviously gave us no pointers to current form but their win over Hamburg did. Any team knocking out the West German champions and the current holders demanded the utmost respect. And Dinamo had gained their win over the Hamburg side just a few months after the West Germans had won the European Cup with a single goal victory over Juventus. At that time the Italians had seven of their own national side as well as Platini from France and Boniek from Poland. The warning signals were there for us.

Dinamo Bucharest had not lost a goal in the three ties they had played on their own ground in the Rumanian capital and so, clearly, it was there we had to watch ourselves most carefully. But equally significant was that they had scored in all their away games – one goal for a win in Finland, two goals in a 3-2 defeat in the Volspark Stadion in Hamburg and then one goal in a drawn game in Minsk. These were the statistics which were available. Until Joe Fagan had them watched there was little more to go on. It is always the same when you face a team from Eastern Europe. It is always a journey into the unknown. Little is written about their players. Little publicity surrounds them. Unlike when you play, for example, a team from West Germany or Spain or Italy or Portugal where so many of the players have been seen so often in big games on television.

So there was not the chance to learn too much about the individual players until the game was on top of us. They came to Anfield like the teams before them had done determined to lose nothing. Or as little as possible. It was a Sammy Lee goal which gave us our win but it was a clash between Graeme Souness and one of their players which captured the headlines and drew threats from the Rumanians of how we would be treated when we went to the second leg. They had looked a really good side against us – disciplined, organised, and with a little bit of flair that sometimes can be missing in teams from behind the Iron Curtain. They were also hard. Tough as nails, in fact, as Graeme found out. But, then, one of their players also learned that Graeme is a hard man to intimidate. He went home with a broken jaw. Graeme went home nursing a few bruises and with his ears still ringing from the threats which the Bucharest players had issued to him on his way off the field!

It was not a return leg we were looking forward to. There was the promise of reprisals from the players. There was the fact that we had a very fragile one-goal lead against a team which had been able to create chances against us at Anfield. Indeed, they had struck the post before Sammy grabbed the goal for us. And they had other chances before and after that too. Both Bilbao and Lisbon had looked formidable hurdles – this was the most cruelly intimidating of all. Poor Graeme was even getting the message from the soldiers at the airport when we arrived. The newspapers there had whipped up a campaign of hate against him. Even though none of us could understand the language I think we all knew from the gestures that they expected to see Graeme flying back home to Liverpool on a stretcher. A broken leg seemed to be the most persistent promise on offer to him.

Lesser players would have wilted under the pressure which

mounted before the match. Not Graeme. He was the coolest of us all. There must have been 80,000 fans crowded into that stadium when we took the field. All of them were booing Graeme. He was the target whenever we went out and all the way through the warm-up. He had only to touch the ball and the boos and the jeers rose to a crescendo. Of course, we simply started to give him as much of the ball as possible just to wind him up and, as I said before, to try to release the tension. A lot of players might have cracked under that kind of pressure. A lot of players would have been hiding a bit. Not Graeme. On one occasion there was a ball played towards him. He went to gather it and bring it down, then as the crowd booed he pulled away and dummied the ball. There they were still booing and he hadn't even touched the ball. It was the cheekiest thing I've ever seen and that said more to the fans than anything. It told them plain and simple: "Boo all you like, you don't scare me."

The message reached the rest of us too. If Graeme could handle that abuse what did we have to worry about? We went on to win 2-0 and it was one of the most satisfying victories we had known in Europe. Not as brilliant as Lisbon but equally memorable in a different way. It was a game which had called for strength of character more than anything else. None of us had ever known such a hostile atmosphere. Yet Graeme showed all of us the way that day and Ian Rush scored twice. Even though they managed to get a goal they never looked like winning. The tension which had been whipped up by the threats, the frenzied backing of the crowd and the whole feeling of ugliness in that massive stadium seemed to react against them. It was almost as if they were more worried about losing than we were. Going through that tie gave all of us the feeling that we could go anywhere and win – even Rome and the Olympic Stadium with the local heroes as the opposition. For even as we were going through the ordeal behind the Iron Curtain, Dundee United manager Jim McLean was suffering the same abuse as Graeme Souness in Italy. The Tannadice boss was crucified by the Italian Press and almost attacked by the Roma players at the end of the match. It gave us a foretaste of what might be waiting for us in the Eternal City. But we did know that Bucharest and its special delights had prepared us for the worst.

Roma had beaten United, a tiny team with a fraction of the Italian side's resources. But they had struggled to do so. They had lost 2-0 at Tannadice and we all knew from television that United might have scored more goals. But then they won 3-0 at home and it was at home over 90 minutes that they had to play to win the European Cup and take it back to Italy for the first time in 15 years.

The penalty drama is over. Liverpool gather round the European Cup which they have just won for the fourth time in their history in Rome.

We realised that there would be a great deal of pressure on the Italians, though playing at home was the kind of pressure we would have found easy to accept and live with. Certainly the expectations placed on their shoulders were going to be great. Everyone in Rome, everyone in Italy, probably everyone in Europe outside Liverpool, looked for them to win. It was natural that supporters should think that way. I know that if we had simply to win a game at Anfield to take Europe's number one trophy then even I would feel pretty confident and I'm usually the most pessimistic person in our dressing-room. While this match was at the municipally owned Olympic Stadium it was still the ground where Roma played their Italian First Division matches. It was the same as San Siro was to the Milan clubs, or the Stadio Communale to the giants of Turin.

But I suppose the experiences that Dundee United suffered alerted us to the fact that we might face problems similar to those in Bucharest. The Romans wanted their team to win. That was natural. But they didn't really care how they won and that could be disconcerting. There is a ruthlessness about the Italian game, a cynicism if you like, and the crowds are particularly intimidating. I can remember wakening up on the morning of the game in our hotel. Someone had put the television on and soon the word went round all the players' rooms: "Switch on the telly on such and such a channel and take a look at the Olympic Stadium." And there it was, hours and hours before the kick-off, packed with the Italian supporters. We were going to play the most important game of the season there, for some of the lads the biggest game of their careers, and we were still in bed while these fans were waiting for the kill! Naturally, we were the victims as far as they were concerned.

Then when we arrived in the team bus we came over the hill and saw the stadium sitting down below us. This was still a long time before the kick-off and yet the ground was three-quarters full – only our fans hadn't arrived to take up their places. The rest were in. They were there to see Italy back at the top in European club football. They had been in the shadows. The national team had won the World Cup but the clubs, in spite of their foreign stars and their huge salaries, had lagged behind. The public did not like that. They wanted to be back on top and this was the best opportunity they had had. It was also a return to glory for Roma who had been eclipsed down through the years by the two Milan teams and by Juventus and Torino. Now, here in the Olympic Stadium, they believed their time had come. I think their supporters saw us as simply coming along to make the game official. They did not see us being able to stop their team.

We saw it all in another light of course. If we could win it then we would draw clear of Ajax and Bayern as the teams who had won the trophy three times. We would take it for a fourth time and that would put us behind only the fabled Real Madrid in the European Cup honours' list. That was important. Then too, we wanted to take the European title in the same season as we won the First Division Championship at home. The first time Liverpool had won the Cup in Rome, coincidentally, against Borussia Moenchengladbach they had won the title. But that had been before my time. Before Kenny's and Graeme's too and we wanted to be able to say we had done that.

We also wanted to win it for Joe Fagan, for he had given a little bit of a hint of what it meant to him when we had won that game in Bucharest. When we had got back into the safety of the dressing-room after our win there Joe had shut the door and then told us all, "Keep calm. This is the time to keep calm." Then, suddenly, as we tried to absorb this advice while we were still so elated, Joe let out a shriek of joy himself. None of us had ever seen anything like that from him before. He was always so quiet, so laid back, that even when you won 7-0 then the most you would be looking for from Joe was a "Not bad, lads". That's just the way he was. He never seemed to allow himself to get too carried away by any result. Then came that shriek which the Rumanians must have been able to hear in their dressing-room. It showed us just how tremendous he felt himself at reaching a European Cup final in his first season as manager. It meant something to him. Something very special. I think that registered with us all and we wanted the trophy for him as well as for ourselves, the club and the fans. Roma were not the only team who would be there on the field believing that they should be taking the trophy home with them. We were going to have a say in that no matter how much intimidation we might have to suffer and no matter how much the home crowd would back them in their mission to restore the club's greatness.

We knew the odds were stacked against us but that was the way it had been every time we had gone away from home that season. The memories of the other games came back to sustain us and when we were going out on to the field to face the 70,000 fans we all burst into song. We walked past their dressing-room and we were singing the Chris Rea hit of the time, *Don't Know What It Was – But I Love It*. They must have thought we were crazy. And I know that the Roma coach, the Swedish legend Nils Liedholm, said afterwards that he could not understand what was happening. He could not grasp how we could be so relaxed.

Looking back I don't know either. Maybe it was just a little bit of whistling in the dark by the lads, maybe just that usual way we had of putting up a front for the opposition. It worked as far as Liedholm and his players were concerned. I think we put the fear of death into them as we went past their dressing-room door. But even though we did win the little bit of psychological warfare the pressure remained very much on us. It was without a doubt the most difficult final we had to play in because of the very obvious fact that Rome were playing at home, as I've already pointed out.

Smoke bombs and flares went off in the stadium before the kick-off and the atmosphere was as intimidating as any I'd known, but then the television pictures hours beforehand had prepared us for all of that. Strangely they seemed more nervous than we were in the early part of the game. Perhaps they had been burdened too much by the expectations of the fans. At any rate, we were able to take the lead after 15 minutes when Phil Neal scored. It was a little bit lucky but it counted and from then until almost right on half time we controlled the match. Then they had the break they wanted and needed. With their fans demanding action, willing them to go forward, and with us knowing that soon the crowd would turn against them, they scored. Little Bruno Conti crossed and their centre-forward Roberto Pruzzo headed into the net. That lifted them as we went off the field at the interval and the boost remained with them as we went back to play the second half. They roared into attack after attack but we handled them and returned to control the game as time was running out on us.

Neither team could score though, and it was the same in the

half-hour extra time. We could not be separated and for all that Roma were playing in front of their own fans and getting the benefit of extra time on their own ground – something clubs always hope for – they didn't come out to attack us. It was almost as if they were happy to wait for the penalty kicks which were to eventually decide the game. That was what they seemed to want. It might seem incredible that a team with built-in advantages would retreat into defence and be happy to head for the kind of shoot-out that most players want to avoid if possible. But that was the impression they gave me and the other lads. In that match, in the later stages of the 90 minutes moving into the extra time, I knew they would never score against us again. They didn't want to make a game of it at all. They didn't want to risk anything to win the game. It was extraordinary. And long before the referee blew the final whistle I knew that, inevitably, the final was heading for a penalty-kick decider. That worried me more than the game had . . . because we had been practising penalties in training and the results had been disastrous!

It was strange, almost as if there had been some kind of premonition that the game would go to a shoot-out. But at the Melwood training ground before heading for Italy and the final the backroom staff had worked on penalty kicks. They had five first-team players taking penalties against the youth team goalkeeper and five youth team players taking penalties against Bruce Grobelaar. The result of that little exercise ended with the youth team winning 5-0. Every one of the first-team men missed and these were the same guys who were to take the penalty kicks in Rome if we had to go to that extreme. Well, here we were at that crisis point and I think every single one of us must have seen action replays of these Melwood misses coming back to haunt us. There had been no messing about in that practice session. They all had been trying to score, really having a go, but they couldn't do it. Alan Kennedy, for instance, must have tried a dozen times and he failed every time. He kept doing the same thing, hitting the ball wide when he tried to place it so carefully in the corner of the net. Alan had missed two penalty kicks previously in pre-season tour games in West Germany and Spain. These were the only two he had taken but he was one of the volunteers. He was desperate to take a penalty. The worrying thing was that he couldn't score. Eventually Joe gave up on him and told him if he had to take one then to hit it in the other corner.

I was not involved in any of this. If penalties were to be taken then I was a certainty to be 36th on the list of potential kickers. I had taken one before, in a tournament in West Germany, and had missed. Actually the keeper made a great save but it's not a job I ever wanted. I would be nervous taking a penalty kick, but it is nothing to do with nerves. It's simply the feeling I have about going up there into the opposition penalty box. I'm lost up there. It's like going into another country as far as I'm concerned. I am a danger if I ever get into the other team's penalty box – a danger to us! I don't get up there too often, thank goodness, but on the odd occasions I do then it's a case of getting rid of the ball just as quickly as possible. I don't want it and I don't want to be there either. So I wasn't in the firing line when the whistle went in Rome. I was out of it and after Melwood I was worried. If Roma were happy to wait for penalty kicks then they clearly fancied their chances of winning the European Cup by that route. To be utterly honest, I was starting to fancy them a bit too.

When it went to penalties no one knew what was going to happen. It was all a bit of a shambles – which is how Stevie Nicol managed to take the first kick and miss it. The practice session had gone so badly that no one really knew what we should do. So Nicol just said, "I'll go first", grabbed the ball and took the kick. When he missed that was us in trouble, especially when they took their first kick and scored. Phil Neal, our recognised penalty-taker, was next and he scored and we were back to level as their World Cup winger Bruno Conti stepped forward for the next try. He followed Nicol's example and sent the ball soaring high over the bar. Graeme Souness took the next one for us. He scored. Righetti for them – he scored. Rushie was next and again we were in front. Their star striker, another World Cup ace, Graziani, was next forward. He looked nervous as he placed the ball, knowing how much depended on him scoring. By this time Bruce, in goal, was moving around, but always keeping his feet still which is all a goalkeeper has to do when a penalty is being taken. The Italians didn't like it, probably it increased the nervousness Graziani was feeling and he hammered the ball over the bar too.

The European Cup is won again, this time in Rome as Joe Fagan holds the trophy surrounded by his Anfield stars.

Now we had one kick left and so did they. But if we scored then the European Cup was going back to Anfield again. Alan Kennedy was the man who was last of our five kickers and once more memories of Melwood flooded back – all those tries Alan had had and all those misses which had resulted. But what Alan was remembering was Joe Fagan's advice."Hit it in the other corner," Joe had said. "And side foot it," he had added. So Alan who had never scored with a penalty before had our European Cup fate in his hands and he remembered Joe, did what he had been told on the training ground and scored. It was taken just as Joe had suggested. Alan had learned his lesson well. So well that we had taken Europe's number one trophy again.

It was a great moment for all of us. I can still remember before going out for the extra-time period Joe Fagan coming round and speaking to us all. He was saying, "Lads, you have done great. You have done brilliantly for the club, for the fans and for yourselves. Just hold your heads high in the extra time because it doesn't matter about the result now. You have done enough."

He kept on saying that, saying it didn't matter, and we began feeling, "It does matter." There was no way we wanted to lose that game after going so far and through so much. Joe got us feeling that way, he wound us up and it worked again. Good old Joe, I thought later. He worked it on us again, the old Liverpool way had won.

Roma had not been the greatest team we had met but given all the circumstances surrounding that final the victory gave me more satisfaction than any of the others. The glory that was Rome . . ..

CHAPTER TEN

The Horror of the Heysel

THE FULL HORROR of what happened in the Heysel Stadium on that May night in 1985 was hidden from all of us until after we had played in that tragic European Cup final against the Italian champions Juventus. And even then it was so great that we seemed unable to accept the grim news of the deaths which had occurred on the old and crumbling terraces of the Heysel Stadium in Brussels. Now, today, looking back on that evening I find it difficult to relate to the events which brought death to so many people who had gone there to see a football match. There is a numbness whenever anyone raises the subject. It seems to come back to haunt you over and over again and there is nothing you can do to rid yourself of the memory of that terrible night.

I don't think any of the players who took part in that game will ever escape from the tragedy which happened. I've never wanted to look at the game on a video tape which a friend made for me. It has remained unopened because I know that I could not face watching the events which have overshadowed everyone at Liverpool from that day onwards.

It was a tragedy for all of those people who died and for their families and friends. It was a tragedy for the Juventus players who, though they won the European Cup, must have felt as saddened as we did. And it was a tragedy for Liverpool Football Club who had been so jealous of their reputation in Europe and who saw that reputation left in tatters after the events in the Belgian capital.

When the memories do come back there is a constant sense of unreality about them. It's as if my mind has tried to reject the events at Heysel. And I don't really know if that has happened to me since the tragedy of whether it affected me at the time when the full scale of the death toll finally reached us. It is as if a part of my mind has been saying: "This didn't happen." But, of course, we all know it did. Still, though, none of us can quite grasp how it could all have happened and how it was allowed to happen. In the light of what we eventually did learn I think we would all agree that it could have been, and should have been, avoided. Just too many things went wrong, too many people died, because too many mistakes were made.

I can recall what may have been the first little hints of trouble – but then I'm looking back at the events with hindsight. We had gone out to take a look at the pitch and get the feel of the atmosphere in the stadium about an hour and a half before the kick-off. It was the usual way of doing things at Liverpool, and as a club they believe in sticking by a tried and tested formula. But, this time, just as it had been a year earlier in Rome when we won the Cup on penalty kicks, we didn't get the chance to walk across the pitch to test its condition. On each of these two occasions there were youngsters playing in games as a warm-up to the final. All we could do in each case was walk around the track and wave to the area where our own supporters were to be placed. To get to that section of the ground we had to walk past the area of Italian support where the tragedy occurred. We had to stay very close to the inside perimeter of the track, skirting the field closely because we daren't go too close to those Juventus fans. There were missiles being thrown at us as we walked along and among the missiles were chunks of stone which we now realise came from the terracings which were

falling apart. When we did get to our own support the area
looked overcrowded, and this was next to the Italian section.
You did not need to be an intellectual or an expert on football
crowd control to see that the seeds of trouble were all there.
You had a mix of volatile Italians, plus equally volatile
Liverpool fans lodged at the same end of the ground. The
normal situation was that fans were kept as far as possible apart
– usually that meant at opposite ends of the ground. This time
that type of organisation was non-existent.

A Merseyside duel – and Hansen comes in to tackle Bob Latchford of Everton.

Later we were to find that thousands of fans who had made
the trip to Belgium without a ticket had been able to get into the
ground. The turnstiles had been undermanned and the few
thousand who had travelled in hope, but who were ready to
watch the game on the telly if a ticket didn't turn up, were able
to get in. It was a recipe for trouble and I felt uneasy as I went
back into the dressing-room. I'm not suggesting for a moment
that I thought that anything would happen on the scale of the

tragedy which did occur but I did have the feeling that there could be trouble between the rival sets of fans, that there could be skirmishes, and that was something that Liverpool as a club had always tried to avoid. I doubt if any club has ever been as proud of its good reputation and of the lack of trouble at its European games.

Maybe if some of the stringent precautions which had been taken by the French authorities when we won the European Cup in Paris against Real Madrid four years earlier had been followed, then the whole nightmare could have been avoided. That year the French police had been out in force all along the routes leading to the Parc des Princes. My father was there and he had told me all about it, as did a whole lot of other fans who had made the trip. No one was allowed near to the stadium without being in possession of a ticket. And if anyone tried to argue, then they were dealt with by the riot police and those sticks they carry. They stood no nonsense and the atmosphere outside the ground that night was apparently frightening. In Rome the previous year the security had not been tough but it had still been superbly organised. The Heysel didn't come close to either of the previous games as regards the standards of security required at top European games today.

However, once back in the dressing-room, we started to prepare for the game, and I remember Kenny lying on a bench because he was feeling ill. The players were all scattered about the room because the dressing-rooms at the Heysel are huge and you felt lost in them. Then the first suggestion that things were going wrong arrived when someone came into the dressing-room to say there had been trouble. I can't remember who it was who came in first, whether it was one of our party or whether it was an official of the European Union. From then on it was chaos. Rumour followed rumour: this had happened; that had happened; and, inevitably, as you tried to piece together all the different garbled stories which were arriving in the dressing-room then the more confused the entire situation became.

I can remember leaving the room at one stage and going into

the tunnel in an attempt to find out for myself, to see with my own eyes, if you like, what was happening. Two Italians came screaming at me and someone told me a wall had collapsed. But because of the wire mesh over the tunnel there was no way that I could see anything.

The next we knew was that the start of the game had been delayed. But that came as a bald statement. No reason was given as to why there should be a delay, and any questions we tried to ask were ignored. No one told us anything. I sat there and started playing cards with Alan Kennedy, who was in the dressing-room with us, even though he was not even on the subs' bench that night. It was one way of trying to escape from the tension which was building all around. And still muddled story after muddled story found its way into the dressing-room. Someone would appear to tell us one thing and within minutes someone else would tell us another. One would say there was trouble, another would tell you everything was fine and the game was ready to start.

But an official silence prevailed – and was to prevail until everything was over. My wife was out there in the crowd. My dad was there too but I never felt at any time during this agonising wait in the dressing-room that there was anything to worry about. We were kept so far away from the trouble that it could have been happening a thousand miles away from us instead of right there in the same stadium.

The first we had of any *real* news, I mean news that we could trust, was when a UEFA official came in to ask our captain Phil Neal to go out into the ground to talk to our supporters and ask them to calm down. Then we knew that there was trouble – but still we didn't know the extent. The rumours had gone from ten dead to 20 dead, to no one dead at all. We even heard that the kids who had been playing in the warm-up game had all been killed when they left the field to move on to the terracing.

It was only when Phil Neal came back that we did realise that people had died out there and he thought that the game was going to be cancelled. There seemed to be so much confusion then, because within minutes of being told that, we were then being told to get ready to take the field as the match was going ahead.

I remember going out and seeing that a wall had collapsed. I remember looking into the stand for a glimpse of my wife – not that I was worrying about her safety, but just to give her a wave. I did that, then I looked over to the rubble at the side of the pitch and I knew something had gone terribly wrong. But I wasn't able to grasp just what had really happened. The game was nothing. It meant nothing. Not to us, and not to them. Footballers can often be blamed, like other sportsmen, for concentrating too much on their own sport and ignoring what is happening around them. I don't think anyone could say that this time. The biggest prize in European football was at stake but you would never have known it. Both teams just wanted to get the game out of the way. We went through the motions for 90 minutes, all of us knowing that something which overshadowed anything which might happen during the game had already occurred.

I can understand people who thought it was wrong to play the game. That decision was out of our hands anyway. That was up to the match organisers and probably to the local police authorities. But looking back, even though the 90 minutes remains a horrific memory for me and probably for everyone else who had to play in the game, it was the right decision. Who can say what kind of trouble might have followed if they had made up their minds not to play the match? That could have sparked off further trouble – something the organisers wanted to avoid at all costs.

No more risks could be taken on that dreadful night, and even though it meant that the game had to be played with a backcloth of death it still had to go ahead. Don't ask me for details of the game. I know that Michel Platini scored with a penalty and I know that they won the European Cup. I also know that, like ourselves, they didn't care who had won. Even afterwards in the dressing-room we huddled around in little groups because now, *and only now*, we were learning the true horror of the night. It was then we learned how many people had died and how it had happened. It was then we learned the full details of the Heysel tragedy. And, again, when we thought about the result we also thought, "Who cares?"

A dramatic moment at Anfield as Alan Hansen is up helping his attack in a game against Norwich.

Then, after that, we heard more. We heard the personal details. We learned of the other lives which had been affected by the tragedy and the happenings all around the stadium. For instance, there was my own sister-in-law whose stand ticket was at the end of the stand right above the wall where the collapse occurred. She saw it all. The whole thing. For months she couldn't sleep because the memories of that moment when the wall came down returned to haunt her. Like all of us she will never be able to forget the Heysel Stadium. And there was Paul Walsh's girlfriend, who was grabbed by a gang of Italian fans and dragged over and forced to look at the dead bodies where the medical teams had piled them up. That frightened all the

wives who were there, sitting together, because they believed
there might be reprisals attempted against them. How can
anyone recover from that kind of experience? How will she ever
be able to forget the Heysel Stadium? Also, there were the club
officials, the men who were being held responsible in some
quarters but who, if they had been asked to organise the game,
would have been able to avert the tragedy. The chairman John
Smith and the secretary Peter Robinson had pleaded with the
match organisers for weeks beforehand to keep the rival fans
apart. No one listened. They had wanted to get the ticket
allocation properly set up. No one listened. How can these
people ever be able to forget the Heysel Stadium?

Over the years Liverpool were paranoid about avoiding
trouble in European games. Even when we got tickets from the
club for away games we had to be able to give assurances as to
whom the tickets were intended for. If the organisation had
been left to Liverpool the tragedy would have been avoided.
I'm certain of that.

That didn't happen. Peter Robinson was a voice in the
wilderness when the plans were being drawn up before the
final. And since then Liverpool Football Club has been in the
European wilderness along with every other English club. That
is the Heysel hangover, the legacy, if you like, for the game in
England. I am not going to attempt a whitewash of our
supporters. We know that they were involved in the terrible
things which went on – but we have also heard of the
provocation many of them were put under. Not that there can
be any excuse for anyone when deaths of so many innocent
people have occurred. But there is little doubt that the
organisation fell far below the standards set at previous
European finals and that parts of that stadium were in
disrepair.

Nevertheless, the ban on Liverpool was made, and it
effectively ended my career in that area. I feel sorry for the
players who have not yet been able to play in Europe. Their
skills are not being tested against the best players in the world.
They are not getting the opportunity to match themselves

against the stars who play in Italy and Russia, in West Germany and Spain, in Rumania, in Portugal and in Poland. The ban has hurt the club – which was surely the intention of the European Union disciplinary committee, but it has also hurt the players and it has possibly affected the standards of the game in the First Division. We are left assessing ourselves only against the players we know so well. The element of surprise, the tactical variations which are used by different countries, the innovations which have so often come from the Continent, are missing. That cannot be good for the long-term development of the game.

Ian Rush is an onlooker here as Alan tries a shot for goal in a First Division clash.

I hope that the European Union will soon lift the ban, allow English clubs back into Europe and make the target for their anger the troublemakers among the fans. Hammer them. Make them pay for the trouble they cause. If necessary, keep them away from matches being played on the Continent – but give the clubs and the players a chance again to take part in the greatest club games of them all.

Even a comeback, though, would still only ease the pain for those players who were in Brussels. No one who was there will ever be able to forget the Heysel Stadium. It will remain a recurring nightmare for thousands and thousands of people.

CHAPTER ELEVEN

A Double Win – and then a New Team

WHEN YOU STUDY the Liverpool approach to things there is one aspect which always strikes me – the way they regularly recruit top names. Not when the club may be struggling, but often when the team is at the top. They have a seeming belief that the best time to strengthen a team is when the team is already strong. Maybe that's why they have had unrivalled success in the years I have been with the club and before that too.

No one has been able to dominate the game the way Liverpool have done. There have been flurries from opposition clubs, little bits of success here and there, but nothing has been sustained the way Liverpool have sustained their winning ways. And, always, when a Liverpool team looks as if it is about to break up then the management have always had star replacements ready. When Kevin Keegan decided to make a career move to the Continent and join Hamburg the fans thought he was going to be irreplaceable. Bob Paisley, though, made a car journey north to Glasgow and signed Kenny Dalglish. With all due respect to Kevin he was never missed. Dalglish became one of the club's greatest players.

Liverpool are never slow to move into the market place and you have to admire the way they go about their business. There is little of the ballyhoo and fuss which some managers make when they are trying to sign a player. They try their best to keep things quiet. The return of Ian Rush, for instance, was the most secret deal football has ever known. No one had any inkling that Rushy was to be allowed to leave Juventus. No one had the slightest idea that Liverpool were ready to bring him back. If anyone had known there would have been a queue of top managers trying to buy him. Kenny Dalglish had the deal set up before anyone else could even consider moving in. It was the same when Kenny signed himself. Bob Paisley set up the move with the late Jock Stein and the transfer was finalised quickly and quietly one night at Celtic Park.

The way they do business is typical of the whole club and of their approach to the game. Apart from the great Bill Shankly no one has ever made outrageous boasts or promises about what Liverpool are going to do. Or about what they have accomplished. That is frowned upon. They don't do it because they don't like it. And I suppose they don't do it because they have seen it backfire at other clubs where too much talk has put too much pressure on the players. And too high expectations have possibly destroyed a team's chances.

If you remember there was the time when Crystal Palace, then managed by Terry Venables, were being hailed in London as the brightest young team of all, the team who would take on Liverpool and the rest. They were dubbed the team of the 'eighties when they came to Anfield. It was still only 1979, though. We beat them that day and their challenge petered out. Bob Paisley allowed himself a little laugh at the end when he told the Press: "We were just making sure that they weren't going to be the team of 'seventy-nine . . .". It was a typical Paisley comment, one which didn't sneer at the opposition or comment on their approach or professionalism but simply put Palace's London boosters quietly in their place.

Palace is just one club from London – or from the entire south – who have been boosted beyond their accomplishments by the capital Press. But for all the time I have been at Anfield there has never been any really sustained challenge from down there. In the years I have been with Liverpool there have been a lot of good players and good teams from London but the only really sustained challenge over a period of years has come from Everton. They are the only team who have been able to stay at the top for a three-year period – apart, of course, from ourselves. To a large extent titles are won away from home – that's where it's hardest. We have found it difficult to get points

Another trophy marks another Liverpool milestone and memory for Alan Hansen as he clutches the FA Cup – the one which almost got away!

in London. Going down there has provided us with problems but we have been able to overcome them on a whole number of occasions. It has been said that the London derby games worked against the clubs from the capital because there are so many of them. But I'm convinced that if the Liverpool teams I have played in had been based in London we would have enjoyed the same success.

Most titles are won, or lost, in the vital Easter period. There are extra games then, and tough games then, and so in the months of March and April you can see which way the title is heading. That is the real nitty-gritty period of the challenge and it's then that you can sense some of the teams wilting. It's all about bottle then and if you don't have it then you won't take the First Division flag. I used to talk to John Wark about the time when he was at Ipswich. They had a powerful team and set up an equally powerful challenge for the championship over two seasons. They finished second each time, behind Aston Villa once and behind ourselves the following year. He used to admit when we talked that they should have taken the title at that time – but they froze. When it came to the real crunch they faded – and that has been the story with every southern team who have offered any kind of challenge in the years I have been with Liverpool.

Of course, Manchester United have threatened, too, but again they have never been able to mount a long-term battle for the title. Unless you count last season when they ended up nine points adrift of us! I feel that United suffer from the fact that they have not won the title for such a long period of time. The last time they were successful was the year after England won the World Cup, when Denis Law and Pat Crerand and George Best and Nobby Stiles were all playing for them and I was still at school in Sauchie. But somehow, year after year, their support builds up the dream that United are going to win it this year. Every season seems to be the same – *this is the year*. And so far not one of the years has brought success. Yet the fans push these dreams on to the players and sometimes I think the burden they have to carry is too much for anyone to bear. In

Ray Clemence – and Hansen himself could have been the target for this bit of advice from the former Liverpool goalkeeper.

1985-86 they had a great start to the season — ten wins in succession — and suddenly we were being told this was the greatest club side England had had in years. They were going to sweep everything before them; this was to be the return of the glory years at Old Trafford. At the end of that season they did not finish in the top three clubs in the First Division. We won the League and Cup double. The claims made for them didn't come out of Old Trafford and they were farcical. No boasts should be made until a team has really achieved something. That's the way we have been taught to act at Liverpool and maybe it's something that others should take on board. It may sound like a managerial cliché to "take each game as it comes" but that has been the Liverpool attitude since I joined the club. It has worked well in those years and it's still working now.

Looking back there have been some victories which have meant more than others to me. Some successes which stand out in my memory rather than the rest . . ... For example, the first title I played any significant role in helping Liverpool win. That was back in 1978-79 — and there was no indication in the early part of the season that we were going to be able to take the title the way we did. Our League start was good but we dropped out of the European Cup we had won the previous spring when we lost to Notts Forest in the first round. Then in the League Cup we also lost. This was to Second Division side Sheffield United and so before September was finished we were knocked out of the two Cup tournaments. It was not what we wanted; not what the club was used to; not what they were ready to accept. And so, gradually, we dug in and made the title our major target. We were undefeated at Anfield that season in the League. In 42 games we lost only 16 goals — and we also scored 85. Eventually we took the title by eight points from Forest at the time when it was still only two points for a victory.

That was an incredible team to play in and a marvellous defence to be part of. I played in 34 League games that season and the recognised first choice defence had Ray Clemence, Phil Neal, Phil Thompson, myself and Alan Kennedy, who had been bought from Newcastle United in the close season. I think that record of goals against will stand forever. No one can ever get close to that again – and there I was, a part of a record-making defence, and still a youngster. I was being coached through the games by the players round about me.

Arrival in triumph at Liverpool Airport with the FA Cup – at last! Skipper Hansen holds the trophy with Manager Kenny Dalglish on the left.

Clem helped me more than anyone in these early days. When I first came into the team he used to look out for me all the time. He was a superb organiser of the defence – I doubt if there has been anyone better. It was an education for me to play in front of him. He used to pull me about, back and forward in that penalty area telling me where I should be placed for certain situations. If I went maybe two yards too far in one direction, then he would tell me immediately and haul me back into line.

When I first went in I was all over the place. Without him I would have been in trouble. But he had patience and he had this knowledge and he was ready to help younger players. He made things come easy for me and I'll always be grateful to him for what he did then.

It's hard to believe now how raw I still was that season but the club had faith in me and the players helped me. I had Clem behind me keeping me right and I had Phil Thompson alongside me. He was looking out for me too. It was an education I would never have gained at any other club. I know that people often say that it doesn't matter which club you go to, that if you are a good player then things will be OK. I don't entirely go along with that view. I know just how much the other players guided me in my early days in the team. That kind of experienced help around you would not have been available anywhere else. Tommo was easy to play with. Like Terry Mac he was often underrated, yet he had a tremendous touch and he was a brilliant passer of the ball. No one ever gave him enough credit, either with us or with England. He may not have been the fastest player in the world – in fact, I used to say my missus could run faster – but with his ability he didn't need pace. He could read the game and he could use the ball and he was an outstanding player for England and for us. He was a natural central defender and Bob Paisley used to always say that it was a specialised position and I would agree with that. I don't honestly think that England have ever really replaced him at the heart of their defence. He was magnificent in the World Cup finals in Spain in 1982 and right now if he was still playing he would be the perfect foil for big Terry Butcher. He would just tuck in beside him and he would be ideal. I played alongside him long enough to appreciate his skills.

The two of them, Clem and Tommo, helped me so much. And that kind of guidance cannot be beaten. You are getting it for 90 minutes of every game as well as on the training ground and it's better than all the theory that can be talked. It was a practical grounding and it made me a Liverpool player. Which is what the club wanted.

As one of the survivors from that time – the manager apart – I still retain a great affection for these players. And an admiration for them too. It was the best Liverpool team I have played in – and I say that with respect for the team we have now. And for the team which gave us the double in Kenny Dalglish's first season as manager.

The captain with the Championship trophy – Alan Hansen shows the First Division prize to the Kop.

I suppose it all seemed fresh to me. Within two years I had a European Cup medal and a First Division Championship medal – and I had never won anything at senior level before. It was a whole new world then and there I was a part of it, playing alongside some of the greatest players in the game. It's hard to tell just how much these heady moments of success meant to me. As well as learning, as well as winning – I was just having a really good time. It was hard to believe that it was all happening to me! But the record books and my own memories tell me that it has all happened and it has continued with amazing regularity in the years since.

The "double" was another important milestone for me and, I suppose, for Kenny too. The one prize which had eluded us had been the FA Cup. Somehow it had seemed as if there was a jinx on us. Then, in Kenny's first year as boss, there it was. Not only did we win the Cup but we also managed to take the title too. It was an incredibly good season for us because of that Cup victory to go along with the First Division title. It stays a special season for me.

It was after all supposed to be a season of transition for us – and a season when the club had to regroup and regather its resources and its collective strength after the Heysel Stadium disaster. Joe Fagan had gone and Kenny Dalglish was taking over as manager. Soon after that, as I've explained in the earlier chapter, Phil Neal and Alan Kennedy had also gone as Kenny stamped the team with his own personality. The previous season Everton had taken the title and while it was good for the city that two teams should be at the top – we didn't want them to think of this as a habit. They proved to be our most persistent challengers that season, too, after the collapse of Manchester United. In the end it was a last gasp win for us. We had to go to Chelsea and win the game there at Stamford Bridge, never the happiest of hunting grounds for us, to take the title. It was Kenny Dalglish who scored for us there and we took the title by two points – and now we had to face Everton, again, in the Cup final and hope that we could end our jinx. At first, in the early stages of the game, it didn't look as if that was possible. It looked, in fact, as if there really was a Cup hoodoo working on the club. After half an hour Gary Lineker escaped from my marking to give Everton the lead and from then on until half time we were under severe pressure as our fans on the Wembley terracings must have wondered if we would ever be able to win the Cup!

Then in the second half Ian Rush scored twice, Craig Johnston scored another and with these goals we made sure of the double and certain, too, there was no way back for our Merseyside rivals. As a managerial debut for Kenny it could not have been bettered. Only three other teams this century had managed the League and Cup double – Tottenham in the 'sixties and Arsenal in the 'seventies. Now in the 'eighties it was our turn. How good that felt . . ..

The captain takes a bow at a packed Anfield before being presented with the League Championship trophy. His Liverpool team-mates applaud Alan Hansen on to the field.

The next season, though, was one of disappointments – for all of us. Maintaining that success was hard. We didn't manage to achieve the same level of performance all the way through the season and so we had to take second place to Everton in the First Division, accept runners-up medals when we lost to Arsenal in the Milk Cup final and face up to a third-round knockout from Luton in the FA Cup. That came after a second

replay and it hurt us badly. Then, after all that gloom and the
feeling of let-down, Kenny Dalglish began, once more, to build
another Liverpool team. Ian Rush was going to Juventus and
with the money from that deal the manager set off to buy a
group of the most talented players ever to play at Anfield.

   We were all aware that the departure of Rushy was going to
be a blow – but John Aldridge had arrived before then and
while Aldo might not have had the most glamorous background
with Oxford I think all of us who had played against him
recognised that he had that knack that Rushy had – he simply
scored goals – often. He was to prove that the following season
when he was top scorer in the First Division with 29 goals – 26
of these coming in the League as we won another title.

   But the gaffer had not stopped buying there. With the Rushy
cash available he bought two outstanding players within five
weeks of each other in the summer . . . John Barnes was first
and then he was joined by Peter Beardsley. Now, there were
people who doubted John Barnes as a Liverpool player. They
tried to say that his "work rate" was not good enough for
Anfield. There were suggestions that he was too much of an "in
and out player" for the Liverpool fans ever to take to. They
were all wrong – and I would have forecast that. When he
played at Watford John Barnes used to always give us
headaches simply because he is such an exceptional player. If
the boss had asked me whom he should sign – then Barnes
would have been the player I would have mentioned before
anyone else. I used to hate playing against him. He gave me a
hard time. He gave us all a hard time and now it's a joy to sit
back there in defence and watch him provide headaches for
other people. He has been a magnificent player for the club and
if anyone doubted Kenny's judgment then I hope they will own
up now. The boss was right . . .. He was right with Peter
Beardsley too. Again he chose a class player, someone who had
been through the mill at club level and at international level.
Peter had known hard times in the First Division and come
back from them in his time with Newcastle. In Mexico in the
World Cup he had been a great player for England and it was

Liverpool team mate Gary Gillespie who has now broken through to the Scotland team.

there when you saw him matching his skills with the best players in the world that you realised just how much talent he had. In the first season these three players had together you knew that the opposition were in trouble whenever John had the ball. He simply had to get down the line and get the ball into the middle and there was the twin threat from Aldo and Peter. Frightening! Absolutely frightening for any defender in the First Division.

But the boss didn't stop there – he went back to Oxford and he signed Ray Houghton, a midfield player who had caught my eye when he played for the Republic of Ireland against Scotland in the European Championships. Again it was an outstanding talent and it was our turn to be dubbed the "team of the decade" or whatever. The "best team in Europe" was one title – but all of them were dismissed as we aimed for the long unbeaten run which was to set us up as champions. We went 29 games without defeat in the League, equalling the record which had been set up by Leeds United back in the mid-'seventies. That was when Don Revie was in charge of the talented team which included Billy Bremner, Jack Charlton and the rest.

It was against Everton that we finally lost. Just 1-0 to a goal from their striker Wayne Clark. That was in March and it came too late to allow anyone to come in to take the title away from us. It was an astonishing run and yet, quite honestly, we never talked about it. No one was saying: "We are on a record run." No one was worrying about when it would end. It's just not the way things are done at Liverpool. It's not a question of staying unbeaten for a long, long time if at the end you are going to finish up empty-handed when the trophies are being handed around. Liverpool is about winning Cups and Championships and this time round we looked set for the double. The Everton defeat and the fact that we did not set up a new record is maybe a disappointment now – but, at the time, it wasn't any big deal. It was a defeat and we had to shrug it off and get on with the rest of the season. That's what we did – and we lost just one more game in the League to Notts Forest before the season ended. We won by nine points from Manchester United who had clung to our heels as the campaign neared its climax. But, as well as the points' advantage we also had a goal difference which was *30* goals better off than them. We scored 87 goals in the League – and we lost just 24. Maybe it didn't match that first team I played in but it came so desperately close. And, also, during the season there were games when the football played was brilliant.

Christmas at the Hansen home in Southport shows Alan and his family beneath the tree.

Times when it was better than anything I have ever seen from a Liverpool team. We were able to score so freely and yet give scarcely anything away at the back. This team has a tremendous chance of becoming the best team Liverpool has ever had. They have the opportunity of beating the team I joined, the team where I learned my trade as a Liverpool player. It's just a tragedy that they didn't have the opportunity to test themselves in Europe – then we would all have known just how great the present side is. If they keep going the way they are going then they will be great and I say that without any fear of contradiction from anyone.

Ironically the two teams who handed us our only League

defeats, Everton and Notts Forest, were also two of the teams
we beat on our way to the Wembley Cup final. We beat Everton
1-0 in the fifth round with a goal from Ray Houghton on their
own Goodison pitch. Then in the semi-finals when we came up
against our old rival Brian Clough we won 2-1 with both goals
coming from John Aldridge. We marched on to Wembley as the
biggest favourites in many seasons. The League title had been
assured, we were the team everyone was talking about and we
were to face little Wimbledon and no one gave them a chance.
As so often happens they didn't read that script. Or, if they had,
they decided to rip it up and write one of their own making us
the victims. We did have bad luck when a goal was disallowed
and a penalty missed but Laurie Sanchez scored for them and
who am I to start complaining about another team's victory
celebrations?

It would have been magnificent to skipper the side to another
double. It would have been historic for the club if we could
have done that and it would have shot down all the critics who
have complained about Kenny Dalglish and sniped at him the
previous season when he failed to take us to a trophy win. None
of us had enjoyed that. None of us enjoyed losing to
Wimbledon either – but I put myself in their position and I
could see just how much it meant to that small club. That's why
you won't get me criticising them or moaning about their style
of play. They use a system that suits them and on the day it
suited them so much that we lost and they went back to their
little Plough Lane ground in London to celebrate their first-
ever Cup win. Sure I envied them but I also gave them ten out
of ten for the way they handled their first-ever Wembley
appearance. Good luck to them – that's what I felt at the end.

In the close season, then, I had my injury problems after
Spain and the boss went out to bring Ian Rush home. He had
an unhappy time at Juventus but I know Rushy and I know
how he will bounce back. I never did believe all the nonsense
which the Italians seemed ready to put about that he had lost
his instinct for goals. I played too long with him. I admired the
goals he scored in his years for the club from close range – and I

know what he can do. He hasn't lost that. It's impossible for Rushy to lose that goal touch that made him the best finisher I've ever seen.

Christmas again – but this time at home with his family. Alan beneath the Christmas tree with his son and daughter.

What has happened now is that the boss has added another big gun to the incredible armoury the club already had up front. As I'm writing this Rushy is still settling – when he does the goals will flow and it will be like old times at Anfield. The Italian job, his year-long nightmare with Juventus, will be just a hiccup in his career. It won't change him. It won't alter the fact that he is the deadliest goal machine that the First Division has probably ever known. I admired his courage in going to Italy when he had the chance. I don't know how I would have reacted if I had had that chance – though I know that I would have enjoyed going abroad. It would have been difficult to refuse the kind of money that Italian clubs offer. But even though it would have suited my style I have always felt that there is challenge enough in the English First Division. It makes me laugh when players say that they are going abroad "for the challenge". Graeme Souness said he was going to Sampdoria for the money and that was honest and more players should simply come out and admit that is why they go too. If you are playing at the top of the First Division in the pressure-cooker atmosphere which exists when you are chasing that title then you don't have to look anywhere else for a challenge. It has been enough of a challenge to sustain me over the years at Anfield – and it shows no signs of changing!

Maybe I'm nearing the end of my career but the pressures at the top remain the same and I still welcome them. You think that you can do without the pressure – but then you wonder how it would be if it wasn't there. Maybe you have lived with them for so long that you can't get on too well without them. I don't know yet. I'll find out when I stop playing and I'll find out then, too, how much I want to stay in the game. I feel I would like to stay on. I feel that I have something to offer. After more than ten years at Anfield – and that means ten years at the top – you have some knowledge of the game to pass on. But that's something I'll look at when the time comes. And that isn't quite yet.

Hansen and son Adam – maybe a signing for Liverpool in a few years time?